The Best of Fishing, Hunting, Camping, and Boating in Missouri

The Best of Fishing, Hunting, Camping, and Boating in Missouri

Tips from an Outdoor Enthusiast

Charles J. Farmer

University of Missouri Press
Columbia and London

Copyright © 2004 by
The Curators of the University of Missouri
University of Missouri Press, Columbia, Missouri 65201
Printed and bound in the United States of America
All rights reserved
5 4 3 2 1   08 07 06 05 04

Library of Congress Cataloging-in-Publication Data

Farmer, Charles J.
  The best of fishing, hunting, camping, and boating in Missouri : tips from an outdoor
enthusiast / Charles J. Farmer.
      p. cm.
  Includes bibliographical references.
  ISBN 0-8262-1553-X (alk. paper)
  1. Fishing—Missouri. 2. Hunting—Missouri. 3. Camping—Missouri. 4. Boats and
boating—Missouri. I. Title.
  SH515.F37 2004
  799'.09778—dc22

                                                        2004019924

  ∞™ This paper meets the requirements of the
American National Standard for Permanence of Paper
for Printed Library Materials, Z39.48, 1984.

Designer: Jennifer Cropp
Typesetter: Foley Design
Printer and binder: Thomson-Shore, Inc.
Typefaces: Palatino, Pristina, and Brighton

Dedicated to my dad and all the other dads and moms who take the initiative to trek into the realm of the outdoors. There is beauty in Missouri for boys and girls in the world of fishing, hunting, camping, and boating. There is beauty in life beyond the hustle, the crowded cities, and the stench of bad air and the blaring of loud noise; in the forests and plains there is life! It can't get better than that.

Contents

Johnson's Shut-Ins

Scott Farmer duck hunting

Duck hunters with dog

Decoys and a fine catch

Canoeing on the Jacks Fork River

Wild Primrose, Hercules Glades Wilderness

Cave on Upper Jacks Fork River

An angler captures a bass

Mark Twain National Forest

Dogwood in bloom

Canoeing to the campsite

Deer watch the photographer

Float trip on the Jacks Fork River

Campers gather around the campfire

The Best of Fishing,
Hunting, Camping, and
Boating in Missouri

Introduction

I have traveled the world in quest of the best sites for fishing, hunting, camping, and boating. Some of my favorite places are right here in Missouri. There are more than 900,000 acres of land, 600 lakes and ponds, and thousands of miles of waterways in Missouri to explore. Whether you're a novice or an old hand, there are many recreational opportunities available to you on Missouri's public lands and waterways.

Fishing, hunting, camping, and boating in Missouri make for year-round enjoyment. The state's mild climate, especially in the southern Ozark Plateau, where big lakes, rivers, and streams are plentiful, allows for easy access throughout the seasons.

Missouri's *Conservation Atlas—A Guide to Exploring Your Conservation Lands* came out in 1995 and is a good source of information on sites throughout the state. It includes maps of Missouri counties, along with directions to all Conservation Department areas, and is a useful guide for exploring the state's beautiful and abundant conservation areas. The *Conservation Atlas* is also available on the department's website. You can use the online version to search by county or area, by name of the place you want to visit, by type (for example, wetlands), or by facility (for example, boat docks, hiking trails). It's an excellent source for planning trips or preparing for activities like fishing, hiking, viewing wildlife, hunting, camping, or just strolling through a quiet wooded area. The department's four nature centers have a lot to offer visitors of all ages.

Whether you prefer to spend the day fishing from a boat with no one around to distract you from your solitude or standing shoulder to shoulder onshore with fishermen from all over the region on opening day in one of Missouri's outstanding trout parks, you'll find what you're looking for.

Missouri offers hunters their choice of deer, furbearers, game birds, waterfowl, and turkey (as well as small animals like rabbit and squirrel). For several species there are both bow and gun seasons. Firearms and archery ranges are available for off-season practice. The Conservation Department provides hunter safety classes for new hunters.

Camping can mean settling into an RV park, complete with showers and electicity—even Internet connections—if you're accomodating some reluctant or first-time campers, or primitive camping in the Mark Twain National Forest, where you can pitch a tent, cook over a campfire, and fall asleep to the call of the owl. From your base, you can explore miles of hiking trails on foot or enjoy a ride along designated horseback trails.

If you enjoy boating, ramps are available at many public locations; liveries can provide canoe rentals for float trips as well as transportation to and from the river; or for a family vacation that the kids will remember, you can rent a houseboat on Table Rock Lake for a weekend or a week.

Up to 75 percent of U.S. citizens live in urban/suburban areas. Many people have lost touch with nature, wilderness, and rural life. You will find that if you leave behind the noise, congestion, and stress of urban life for an hour, a day, or a weekend, you'll return to your daily routine refreshed and reinvigorated.

In the following pages I offer stories about some of my favorite outdoor adventures along with tips I've picked up along the way. I hope you will enjoy these stories, and then I hope you will go have your own adventures in one of my favorite places: the terrific Missouri outdoors.

Fishing

My love affair with the outdoors began when I was small boy catching sunfish with a pole, line, bobber, and worm. My dad was not a fisherman, nor was my mother. I was born in the city, but I quickly discovered the joys of fishing. During the summer, my family and I would go to my uncle's bungalow on Greenwood Lake in New York State. Uncle Andy was my first fishing partner; he taught me to fish when I was just eight years old. After that I made my dad a fisherman because at age eight I could not drive our black '47 Plymouth. There were farm ponds and state lakes near our home that were stocked with bass, bluegill, crappie, green sunfish, pumpkin seed sunfish, warmouth and orange-spotted sunfish, and yellow perch. I was eager to get to them, and I figured Dad would soon get the knack of fishing. Several years later, my family moved to Kansas City, Missouri, where I began watching Harold Ensley on television. He was my fishing inspiration and my hero, and because of him I became interested in fishing as a sport.

I tried to get my whole family involved in fishing trips. Mom sometimes went along, and she outfished all of us, reeling in bass and bluegill. My sister, Gail, who's three years younger than me, never cottoned to the idea of digging night crawlers, never mind putting them on a hook. Hoping to convince her that fishing was fun, I vowed to bait her line all the time if she just went with me. That worked for a few weeks. Dad would drive us to our favorite fishing hole and

Author's father

fish alongside Gail and me. I thought she was getting the hang of it, and I was happy to have another partner. But Gail just didn't care for all that goes along with fishing, such as hooking worms and minnows. Soon, it was just Dad and me again.

Before I tried to turn my dad into a fisherman, his summer activity had been mowing the lawn, and when I told him Gail had scrapped fishing for playing with dolls, he looked up to the heavens as if he knew that fishing would once again keep him from lawn care. He did know of a teenage boy who lived on our block and offered a good lawn service at a fair price. Dad decided to use the boy's service. I was happy because that way we could fish more, and Dad was happy because the lawn looked better then ever. Thank the stars.

After that, Dad and I spent our summer Saturdays fishing. Mom packed sandwiches, drinks, and snacks for us, and we put some folding chairs into the Plymouth and drove to a nearby lake or pond. Most of the time my chair was empty as I walked along the water's edge. Dad was content to sit down near the water and cast from the comfort of his lawn chair, replacing the worm on his hook as necessary.

I can still remember the first Saturday we went out. Dad caught a big largemouth bass and several bluegill. I wandered along, casting from different spots, catching bluegill and having a great time. Late that afternoon we drove home with several fish packed in a bucket of ice. As we pulled into the driveway, I jumped out of the car and raced into the house, shouting to Mom to come and see the fish we had caught. Mom was almost as excited as I was when she realized we had brought home supper. I watched as Dad filleted the fish and then Mom breaded the fillets and fried them in butter in a cast-iron skillet. We all sat down at the table. Everyone took a bite, Mom's eyes sparkled, and she said, "This fish is delicious!" From that day on, we enjoyed fishing together. We drove to different lakes and ponds. Some were good; others were not. We found the best waters, where the fish were abundant. Dad had gotten the knack, just as I had known he would, and he told me that bait fish in the water make good fishing. We also learned that deep, cool water is good for fish, while murky lakes and ponds are bad and do not offer good fishing.

Most of Missouri's lakes, rivers, streams, and ponds are clear and healthy—which is good for both anglers and fish. The long-standing tradition of fishing in the state has given citizens a strong regard for clean waters. The Missouri Department of Conservation has a big job to do managing all those lakes, rivers, streams, and ponds. The department checks water quality and fish populations and tries to maintain good fishing conditions at all public sites. It also advises property owners on stocking and maintaining their own private lakes and ponds. The Conservation Department establishes and enforces state fishing regulations. (Copies of these regulations along with various books and helpful pamphlets are available from the Conservation Department. See suggested reading in the back of the book for more information.) Many fishing areas also have special regulations of their own, which should be posted on site on signs or bulletin boards, or you may see brochures. Always be aware of the regulations that apply to the area you're fishing.

Getting Started

If you've never fished before, get some expert advice before purchasing your first fishing rig. Buying a rod and reel, or selecting the right fishing line and lures, can be an expensive and confusing venture, but it doesn't have to be. Do your homework and talk with your local outfitter to get the best equipment for the type of fishing you want to do and the kind of fish you would like to catch. Local retailers are often the best source for finding good places to fish and guide services to get you stared.

A basic shopping list would include
Rod and reel
6- to 10-pound test line
Tackle box
Package of hooks
Package of sinkers
Bobbers
Live bait or lure
Pliers (needle-nose)
Fingernail clippers or small scissors
Fishing license (Permits may be purchased directly from the Department of Conservation or through local ven dors. Be sure to ask for literature on state fishing regu lations when you buy your permit.)

Missouri's premier lakes include Taneycomo, Lake of the Ozarks, Wappapello, Norfork, Clearwater, Bull Shoals, Montrose, Table Rock, Pomme de Terre, Thomas Hill, Stockton, Truman, Long Branch, Smithville, Mark Twain, Longview, and Blue Springs.

Missouri Rivers are also blessed with excellent fishing, and some are known as great sites for certain types of fish. The Big Niangua above Bennett Spring State Park contains trout, rock bass (goggle eye), and catch-and-release black bass. (The term *black bass* is used to describe several types of bass, including the largemouth, the small mouth, and the spotted

Scott Farmer with a largemouth bass at Table Rock Lake

bass. Rules on catch-and-release can vary depending on the location, particularly on impoundments versus rivers. Consult the Conservation Department's fishing regulations.) Big Piney below Slabtown has rock bass and catch-and-release black bass. Rock bass, black bass, and trout can be found in Bryant Creek, which is a fine place to fish and canoe.

The Current River, Eleven Point, Gasconade, and Jacks Fork are the cream of the fishing crop for rock bass, black bass (catch-and-release), trout, and some crappie. James River near Springfield, Missouri, is good choice for catch-and-release smallmouth bass, catfish, rock bass, bluegill, and white bass. The Osage—Bagnell tailwater—is good for fishing for rock bass, white bass, and catfish; the Truman tailwater section is good for fishing for crappie, white bass and hybrids, walleye, and catfish. Fishing is only allowed on certain parts of the river, so observe the "no fishing" signs.

State regulations require that some fish be released no matter where in Missouri they are caught. They are

    lake sturgeon, pallid sturgeon

    harlequin darter, goldstripe darter, crystal darter, swamp
       darter, Niangua darter, refin darter, longnose darter

    taillight shiner, Sabine shiner, Topeka shiner

    spring cavefish, Ozark cavefish

    Neosho madtom, mountain madtom

    cypress minnow, central mudminnow

    flathead chub

In Missouri waters, anglers will find crappie, bluegill, sunfish, bass, catfish, bullhead, trout, walleye, sturgeon, carp, and muskellunge. All these fish have their fans. My favorites are bass, trout, and the elusive muskie. I've spent many hours trying to lure these fish, and I've learned a few things about them, and about people too, along the way. In the following pages, I'd like to share these lessons with you.

The Best Fishing in Missouri, or How to Catch Bass All Summer Long

With all the technical information and sophisticated equipment available to bass anglers these days, it would seem that the black bass simply does not stand a chance against the new breed of supereducated bass lovers. In reality, bass humble us more that we humble them. Sure, we have our good days (and we remember them vividly), but let's face it, even the bass pros get skunked on occasion. I know—I have fished with some of the best of them.

The author fishing at Table Rock Lake

Fishermen read about fishing techniques in books and magazines and watch videos on sure-catch methods and television programs that show them how to become better fishermen. They order equipment from catalogs and online stores. Some fill their heads with so much information that they earn degrees in "bassology." Yet there are days on the lake when they cannot buy a bite. What's the deal? Could it be that our brains are overloaded with technical jargon, when what we need is commonsense fishing instinct and skill? Maybe. Do we really have to pack along four tackle

Jeannie Muller fishing at Table Rock Lake

boxes for a May fishing trip on Table Rock Lake? No! Let's get back to basics and start catching bass, one month at a time. May is perfect!

The month of May produces consistently good fishing at area lakes like Table Rock, Bull Shoals, Stockton, Pomme de Terre, Truman, and Lake of the Ozarks. No two lakes are the same, of course, and some techniques that work on one will not work on another. But the methods described here are broadly effective.

Every May, after turkey season, I spend most of my weekends fishing Table Rock Lake. While the James River arm can and does yield good fishing, I prefer the clear waters of the main lake from Joe Bald to Table Rock State Park. The reason for this preference is simple. May is the best month to sight fish, and I have discovered that the main part of the spawn occurs during the first two or three weeks of the month.

In the vast lake area described, it doesn't make much difference where you launch your boat. There are a multitude of spawning coves and back bays to choose from, and all of them hold bass. The water I fish is rarely over ten feet deep. Often the most productive spots are five feet deep or less. Some coves are studded with dead pole timber; others have no visible structure. The best way to fish in these spawning coves is from the bass boat with a bow-mounted electric positioning motor. The approach needs to be slow and quiet. The first three hours of daylight, when the water is generally the calmest, is prime time. If the sun is shining, enhancing underwater visibility, Polarized sunglasses will help you spot reflection and movement in the water. Cloudy, calm days can be equally productive with the fish finning above the water.

Once you have chosen a spot, the method is simple, the results extraordinary. Use a six- or a six-and-a-half-foot light- or medium-light-action graphite spinning rod and a reel loaded with six-pound test monofilament line. The relatively light line is a must for fishing clear water. It is also essential for casting a four-inch balsa Rapala floating minnow, which I find is the best lure. Attach the lure to the line with a small snap (not a snap swivel) to maintain an effective side-to-side and diving action. This flashy dying-minnow duplication triggers plenty of strikes. I have seen bass rise from ten-foot depths to attack the bait. A Rapala with silver sides, black back, and white underbelly is the color combination that has worked best for me.

There are several ways to work the bait. Cast out beyond the nest or area where the feel nests are located. Let the lure rest on the surface for a few seconds. There are times when bass engulf a resting plug. Other times twitching your wrist so that the plugs jumps, either on the surface or underwater, draws a response. Sometimes that slight flick of the wrist, and the slight jump of the lure, is all that is needed for the desired action, but spawning bass will also follow a bait back to the boat before attacking it. More than once, I have found success after vigorously jerking the Rapala nearly all the way to the boat. Apparently, bass regard the "panic retrieve" as the possible loss of an easy meal, or they are acting on an instinctive predatory impulse and nothing more. Whatever the reason, the method works. This brand of bassing lasts two to three weeks. Although short-lived, sight fishing is surface action at its best.

With sight or sound fishing comes a responsibility to the fish and the resource. Since fishing pressure has increased on our Missouri lakes, the catch and release of all spawning fish is the right thing to do in many applications. Immediate release at the catch site insures survival and bass for the future.

Good Catch-and-Release Techniques

Using barbless hooks, or crushing or filing off the barbs on hooks, aids in the quick removal of the fish from the line. This allows for less handling of the fish and its quick return to the water.

Always remove hooks with pliers or forceps.

If a fish swallows the hook, or the hook seems to be stuck in the fish's stomach or throat, cut the line, do not remove the hook. Many hooks will eventually rust or will work themselves free.

Be gentle. Take the time to learn proper fish-handling techniques. Fish should not be squeezed or dropped.

Be sure to keep fingers out of the fish's gills and eye sockets.

Carefully return the fish to the water. If the fish does not take off immediately, gently cradle it in your hands, slowly moving it back and forth until it wiggles and shows signs of being ready to be released.

From shallow spawning banks, bass disperse to deeper water. However, a different kind of topwater action can be enjoyed through the remainder of May and well into June. It requires a heavier line and lure. The Zara Spook, a plastic-bodied plug that is both larger and heavier than the Rapala balsa minnow, is an old-time Heddon Company bass plug that has enjoyed revitalized popularity in the Ozarks. The bait is best cast with a six-foot medium-action casting rod and level-wind bass reel loaded with ten-pound test line.

A technique called "walking the dog" is performed with the Spook. The distinctive zigzag action, for which the technique is named, is produced with little practice by cranking the reel and twitching the rod tip in rhythmic sequence. This method is effective for May bass that are suspended off main channel points and along the outside of standing dead timber. As with the Rapala, I have found that it's a good idea to let the plug sit on the surface for a few seconds before "walking the dog" back to the boat. Because of its weight and bulk, the lure hits the water with a loud splash. Sometimes the splash alone triggers an immediate strike.

A common mistake made by anglers fishing the Spook for the first time is setting the hook too quickly. Wait until you feel the bass on the line before triggering. If the fish misses the lure the first time, do not give up. This is a bait that draws repeated strikes. When fishing the outside edge of timber, position the boat as close to the trees as possible. The Spook, when fished in clear water, has excellent drawing power. It is not uncommon for suspended bass to rise fifteen to twenty feet to attack the lure.

I have had success using chrome bodies with blue backs. No doubt the flash of chrome displayed with the movements of walking the dog attracts deep fish. The first few hours of daylight and the last two hours before sunset are good times to fish the Spook. Best action usually occurs when the surface is calm. However, a light surface riffle does not seem to hamper the effectiveness of the lure.

While the Spook is my number-one choice, other surface lures that work well in May include Rebel Pop-R, Chugger, Tiny Torpedo, Jitterbug, Hula Popper, and buzzbaits. Stick baits, with tiny propellers fore and aft, can also be effective.

You can catch bass all summer long on surface baits, but May is definitely the best month.

For information on purchasing gear and expert advice, the following are excellent resources:

Bass Pro Shops: www.basspro.com   hunting, fishing, and boating retail and online store.

Cabela's: www.cabelas.com   hunting, fishing, and boating retail and online store.

REI, Inc.: www.rei.com   retail and online store for fishing, hunting, camping, boating, rock climbing, biking, and adventure travel.

The Night Shift

While you can catch many fish in the hours just after sunrise and just before dusk, May is also the month that a significant number of bass anglers forgo daytime fishing and switch to the night shift. Nighttime bass-fishing methods are used on many lakes throughout the country, but Table Rock Lake has a reputation as one of the best for anglers using these techniques. This lake has a good population of lunkers (bass weighing four pounds or more) with the largest number inhabiting the clear mid- and upper-lake sections where daytime fishing can frustrate the majority of fishermen. When going night fishing, it is important to pick an area of the lake that you know well. Keep the boat's running time to a minimum. The amount of water covered is not as important as thoroughly fishing a relatively small area.

From sunset until dark, fish the coves, banks along the mouths of coves, and pockets of water off the main channel with six-inch plastic worms, jig and frog, or a number of surface plugs. Large half-ounce spinnerbaits with orange or black skirts and single hammered-copper blades catch a large share of lunkers. A three-inch yellow or black pork trailer hook, connected to the main hook, sweetens the offering and catches short-hitting bass. Plastic worms and jigs also work well at night. Cast as close to the bank as possible and use slow retrieves.

Most bass fishermen choose moonlit nights, when it is possible to see and cast without the use of an artificial light. You can tie on lures by the glow of the moon. Some anglers employ special gunwale-mounted black lights and fluorescent line for probing black water. Running lights are required by law, and boating safety at night is of prime importance.

Bass in Transition

June can be a difficult month to catch bass on large area lakes for a variety of reasons. The spawn is complete, and fish disperse to deeper habitats as water and air temperatures rise. In addition, the lakes have received a great deal of pressure from eager anglers during April and May when conditions are supposed to be ideal. By June many bass have been caught and eaten, thus reducing the number of fish available. Yet the angler who changes from spring to summer tactics and adjusts his lure selection can enjoy a productive month. Seeking deeper, more aerated water is one of the keys to success.

This is the time to break out the tube jigs (Gitzits and the like), grubs, plastic worms, jig, and pork. And this is also the time to put to use some of the sophisticated equipment mentioned earlier. There is a big advantage to having a good boat equipped with a paper or LCD fish-finding graph. A depthfinder, or fishfinder, is a sonar device that allows you to "read" the bottom structure, determine depth, and, sometimes, to spot the fish. It can be a big help to an angler. In addition, here are some techniques that will help you catch more fish.

Carolina Rig

As bass become more finicky in June, July, and August, the rigging of plastic worms and lizards become more important. The Carolina rig separates the soft plastic bait and the sinker by a leader that can be as long as seven feet. This is a good rig for fishing deep (twenty to forty feet) structure and reaching the strike zone where most bass are located in the summer months. The heavier than normal bullet sinker keeps the worm or lizard in contact with the bottom. This does not hold true with Texas-rigged plastic baits that often jump or slip over large areas of bottom structure. And because of the long leader, a bass that inhales a Carolina-rigged worm does not feel much resistance and is likely to hold onto the bait longer for more positive hook setting. There are Carolina rig experts who feel the sinker dragging along the bottom, and stirring up clouds of mud or silt, arouses the curiosity of bass and spurs them to strike. It may be that the mud cloud resembles the trail of a crayfish or a minnow.

The Light Touch

As lakes like Table Rock, Bull Shoals, Stockton, and Lake of the Ozarks became older, their bass habitats changed significantly. When the flood basins were first impounded, there were plenty of woody structures such as live trees and vegetation. This type of habitat favored the largemouth bass. As time passed, trees died and woody structures decayed and disappeared. Brushy shorelines gave way to rocky banks. Spotted bass and smallmouth bass populations increased in clear, deep water areas. Largemouth bass numbers declined. The structure of our lakes now resembles that of the canyon and desert waters of southern California, New Mexico, and Nevada—clear, deep and rocky.

Western bass anglers were the first to design tackle, lures, and techniques for catching bass in clear, uncluttered water. Their methods evolved into what is now called "finesse fishing." In a nutshell, finesse fishing is the mastery of deep water structure through the use of light tackle, vertical fishing methods, fish-finding electronics, special baits, and rigging. One of the best books on this subject is *The Complete Guide to Finesse Bass Fishing* by Michael Jones.

Once the mark of a serious bass fisherman was a "hawg stick," level-wind casting reels, six- to eight-pound monofilament, and a variety of tube jigs, grubs, and four-inch plastic worms. When the now-famous Gitzit lure was introduced at Table Rock Lake, its inventor, pro bass angler Bobby Garland, had been using the tube jig successfully for years out west.

Ten years ago, it was rare to find a spinning rod in a serious bass fisherman's boat. Today, most people prefer spinning rods; however, men and women who participate in bass tournaments use casting rods. Ozark anglers have adopted the clear water tactics proven successful by westerners. The pro bass fishing circuit, and the tournament fishermen from Missouri, no doubt played major roles in expediting the process of adopting the techniques. And it goes without saying that to be a successful bass fisherman in the Ozarks, you should employ the techniques of finesse fishing throughout most of the summer. The more prevalent spotted and smallmouth bass fishing becomes in our highland Ozark lakes, the more important finesse fishing methods become.

There are other successful techniques for catching summer bass. They include flipping, trolling, and the use of live bait. A telescoping flipping stick (a heavy-action rod designed for bass fishing) enables a fisherman to pendulum a plastic worm or jig and pig into tight cover. Flipping is precise casting that disturbs the water very little. Mike Russell, a prominent tournament fisherman from Springfield, Missouri, is an expert with a flipping stick. Mike fishes for summer bass during the hottest part of the day. His theory is that high-quality fish are often found in shallow water, holding tight to cover. The day I fished with him on the James River arm of Table Rock Lake we found bass in flooded grass and vegetation. Mike would flip into dense, junglelike cover reflected by shade. The water was less than five feet deep in most spots. This was a real lesson to me. I figured most bass with any sense would get down thirty to forty feet deep in and around the thermocline. My partner caught several keepers from noon until mid-afternoon. Needless to say, he was not timid about casting into tight spots. And when it came to setting the hook, Mike made the boat rock. It was astonishing to watch him catapult three- to four-pound bass out of weeds, brush, and the thorns of honey locust trees.

Orvis Champ from Nixa, Missouri, was one of the most successful bass fisherman on Table Rock Lake. He fished for fun and for the table and was a believer in two techniques that are not allowed in bass fishing tournaments. Throughout most of the year, he vertically fished live minnows with spinning rod and reel or he trolled Big Bomber crankbaits and Nunguesser spoons with casting rods and reels and three-way swivel rigs. Summer or winter, Champ would find most of his fish suspended between thirty and forty feet deep. Orvis Champ was a hero of mine. He taught many young kids the right way to catch fish. He would take them out in his boat and then watch them reel in bass or crappie, and he was as happy about each catch as they were!

Dick Collier, from Springfield, is a premier structure bass angler and an expert with a Lowrance paper graph and light tackle. He incorporates many of the techniques used in finesse fishing. I was fishing with him on a hot day one August when he motioned me to the bow of the boat. We watched the bow-mounted graph as Dick lowered his line and four-inch pad-dletail worm into the water. The paper graph was sensitive enough to pick up the trail of the line. My partner pointed out the "boomerang-shaped" fish showing on the graph at a depth of thirty feet. When his worm reached the desired zone he closed the bail on his spinning reel. "Watch this fish hit the worm," he whispered, pointing to the graph. Suddenly, the boomerang straightened out and struck, and in an instant, Collier set the hook. I watched the fight on the graph as he battled the bass up from the depths. He hoisted the fifteen-inch spotted bass into the boat and immediately released the fish.

Then it was my turn, and I duplicated Dick's "miracle" by watching a fish on the graph strike my worm. I set the hook, and sure enough, I had a bass on. It turned out to be thirteen inches. We caught and released twenty bass that morning as we watched the spots hit our worms. Collier used the bow-mounted electric motor sparingly to keep us over the fish. "Watching the bass hit" was an unforgettable lesson in structure fishing.

Live night crawlers or crayfish work well for catching fish off the points in July and August in twenty to thirty feet of water. With the right bait, and the right tactics, you can catch fish all summer long!

Common Baits and Lures

buzzbait—made up of a leadhead, rigid hook, and wire that supports one or more blades; a topwater bait with large propeller-type blades that churn the water during the retrieve

chugger—topwater plug with a concave head; designed to make a splash when pulled sharply

crankbait—usually a lipped lure that dips under the surface during the retrieve; *lipless crankbaits* are thin, minnow-like lures that wobble during retrieve

fly 'n' rind (also called *jig-and-pig*)—a leadhead jig and a pork rind

grub—a short plastic worm with a weighted jig hook

jig—a leadhead poured around a hook, also has a skirt of rubber, plastic, or hair

loose-action plug—a lure with wide, slow side-to-side movements

spinner bait—a leadhead lure that resembles an open safety-pin with a hook, also has a rubber, plastic, or hair skirt and one or two blades

tail-spinners—compact, lead-bodied lures with one or two spinner blades attached to the tail, and a treble hook suspended from the body

tight-action plug—a lure with short, rapid, side-to-side movement

Missouri Trout Parks

Bennett Springs, Maramec Spring, Montauk, and Roaring River are Missouri's trout parks and have a great presence in the state. Trout fishing started in the parks in the 1930s. The Conservation Department started the trout parks, and it continues to stock them, but the U.S. Army Corps of Engineers manages some of the Missouri lakes and surrounding lands for flood control, hydroelectric power, recreation, and fish and wildlife conservation. The Corps of Engineers plays an important role in conservation in Missouri.

The seventeen large Missouri lakes mentioned earlier may be the cream of the crop for many anglers in Missouri as well as for those who travel to the state for good fishing. But there are many more lakes throughout the state that are well worth fishing but that do not attract many visitors. Wherever you are in Missouri, you can almost certainly find good fishing nearby. Check the Conservation Department's website or ask other anglers for suggestions. (Remember, if you want to fish in a private lake or pond, or in a section of stream that runs through private land, you need the landowner's permission.)

Catching Trout When Others Can't

Whether you fish the state trout parks, Lake Taneycomo, or Missouri's designated trophy trout areas, there is a right way and a wrong way to go about catching fish. The guys and gals who do it the right way seem to catch most of the fish, and more times than not, they get the biggest ones as well. Take, for instance, opening day at one of Missouri's trout parks, Roaring River:

The open siren has just insulted your eardrums and what seems like twenty lines and lures whiz by your fishing hat. Scarcely twenty seconds go by, and already the fishermen on your right and those on your left have fish on their lines. At that moment, you dismiss the question that crept into your mind, "Why didn't I catch a fish on the first cast?" It

Scott Farmer and author, opening day, Roaring River Trout Park,
with #1 and #2 trout tags

is too early to panic, of course. Anybody can catch trout out
of a pool of stockers. Ten minutes later, the shoulder-to-
shoulder line of anglers is thinning out. Some of those on
either side of you limited out quickly and have already headed
back to camp for breakfast. A tinge of anxiety settles into your
brain. You have changed flies three different times and have
yet to excite a rainbow into hitting.

The frustrating part of this type of trouting is that you can
see the fish swimming in the ultraclear water. Most of them
are twelve inches, but every so often a lunker swims by that
shifts your heart into high gear. The three-pounder fifteen
feet away from the bank is holding in a soft, swirling current.
Every few seconds the fish fins slowly right or left to inhale a
morsel of food that only it can see. The trout's mouth opens,
revealing an instant flash of white. You want to put your olive
green nymph in the "white." That's the target zone. Get the fly
down to the right depth and trace it into the snout of that fat
prize. All it takes is line control. Cast after cast misses the
mark. In frustration, you make a hasty presentation, and the
fly line slaps the surface above the trout. With one swish of

its broad tail, the lunker jets to deeper water and disappears. Your confidence ebbs.

At the trout parks, when you are surrounded by anglers of every size and description, the frustration of not catching fish when others are can lead to an escalating sense of panic. When this happens, the fishermen who has lost his confidence tends to move from one spot to another without doing justice to any one location. Lures and flies are changed with greater frequency than necessary, but the results are the same: No strikes. No trout dinner.

At this point, it is time to stop and evaluate the right and wrong of catching state park trout. The formula for success is quite simple. Remember that at one time or another most of us have gotten into ruts that undermine our ability to catch fish. Let's take a look at those anglers who caught plenty of fish—what they did and what we failed to do.

First Hour Success

Whether you can get a position at one of the better fish-holding pools depends on how early you want to get up and stand in the dark until the siren sounds. The best pools are downstream from riffles, or fast water. The middle or tail of the pool holds the most fish. At Roaring River, there is no wading, so you will be staking out a piece of land on the bank, you hope a spot with good footing. While it is possible to catch trout in other sections of the spring branch, the honey pools offer the best chances, at least for the first hour.

Stocker fish in a new environment tend to cluster in large groups and remain there without moving up or down the stream. This grouping behavior stems from life in their former habitat—concrete raceways. The only thing that really excites hatchery-conditioned fish is when pellet food is broadcast over the surface. As the pellets sink, a feeding frenzy ensues. The most important thing to remember, a least for the first hour of fishing, is to select a lure (a fly or a jig) with enough weight so that it sinks at about the same rate as a pellet of food. The lure should be easy to cast and control.

Jeannie Muller trout fishing on a cold day

Presentation

Those who have mastered a fly rod and can make short accurate casts with light baits while standing in a crowd certainly do well opening hour. Be honest with yourself. If you are not that proficient, a spinning rod would be a far better choice at siren time. Here's why.

A fly rod is a tremendous fish-catching tool in the hands of a master. But it may not be the best choice for shoulder-to-shoulder casting in dim light. By all means, pack a fly rod for use later in the day. But for starters, a five- to six-foot ultralight or light-action graphite spinning rod handles the situation better. Simply put, you have more control of your cast and line to the target zone in front of you. This is not the time for a fly rod back cast or the nightmare of tangling fly line and leader with another fisherman's monofilament line. I have done this before, and the resultant mess can cost you twenty minutes' worth of prime time.

Try this technique. To avoid hangups with other fishermen, cast straight ahead and just beyond, not on top of, the main concentration of fish. With the proper line and lure weight, you should be able to swim the jig, spinner, or fly through the fish at just the right depth. Some newcomers fishing the trout park tend to allow the lure to sink to the bottom and then make a retrieve, or they retrieve the bait so quickly it does not get down into the strike zone. Others tend to jig the offering up and down, which often pulls the lure away from trout or makes detecting strikes difficult. When you swim the jig slowly, it descends in a pelletlike manner and is nearly irresistible to a hatchery-bred trout. The swimming method also keeps you in control of line and lure because there is little if any "belly," or slack, in the line. This means when you feel the "tic" of a strike, your hook set is nearly instant. If you do not have good "line contact," trout will often take the bait but reject it before the hook is set.

It is my belief that technique (swimming method and little or no line slack) is a more important consideration in catching park fish than lure choices. In other words, you can be successful with a variety of proven trout baits if you employ the correct presentation. For most anglers, and definitely for trout park novices, the delivery and retrieve is made easier and more effective with the use of spinning equipment.

Lures

Trout park fish are consistently fooled by a wide variety of flies and lures. But again, it is the presentation more than the particular bait that triggers the strike. The two most effective baits in all four trout parks are the lead-headed jig and the trout-size plastic worm.

The single-hook jig, in effective sizes ranging from 1/132 ounces to 1/100 ounces, can be used in both fly-fishing-only and lure zones. If I had but one lure choice to fish all park zones, the jig would win. It can be accurately cast and, depending on the weight chosen, can easily be guided through the proper strike-zone depths. By itself, it has a built-in sinking action that resembles the drop of a raceway food pellet. If you feel that you are taking unfair advantage of the hatchery trout's penchant for Purina, if it is pure, wild trouting you crave, the trout parks are not for you. As for me, I learned to trout fish at Bennett Springs twenty-eight years ago. Since then I have fished for trout worldwide on some of the wildest streams, rivers, and lakes known to man. But I still enjoy Missouri's trout parks as much as ever. It's all in the mind. I have caught plenty of hatchery trout that fought as hard as, if not harder than, specimens born in the Rocky Mountains.

The marabou jig comes in a variety of colors and color combinations. White is excellent for use during the first hour of fishing because of its visibility. Olive green may be the best overall choice because that color signifies food to trout. The next time you fish, watch trout attack specks or patches of olive-colored moss that for one reason or another came loose from the bottom. Clumps of moss hold aquatic insects that trout feed on. Generally, a fish swallows the ball of moss and then spits it out in order to dislodge the food. There are anglers at the parks who tie on olive jigs in the morning and never switch baits. They do, however, commonly change the weight of their lures by tying on heavier jigs or adding split shot to the line. Other effective colors include black, a black-yellow combination, brown, gray, and a red-white combination.

Jigs are by no means the only good choices. A variety of dry and wet flies work depending on the month, water clarity, and water levels. Small, in-line spinners such as Panther Martins, Roostertails, and Mepps can be deadly accurate when the wind is blowing hard and the surface is ruffled.

White spinners are especially good first thing in the morning. Swimming the spinners just like the presentation of jigs is the way to draw the most strikes. It is important to allow the spinner to sink enough so it flashes through the strike zone.

Plastics, including the deadly plastic trout worm, cannot be legally fished in fly-fishing-only zones. But if you are casting in the lure zone, and it's fish you want, there is no better choice. On a number 10 gold hook, a white, cream, lime, pink, or orange worm presented in a swimming technique, as already mentioned, eliminates the need for any other lures. Weight the worms with miniature split shot to carry them through riffles as well as deep pools. The water zone halfway between the surface and the bottom is commonly fruitful.

Plastic or fur imitation salmon eggs in pink, orange, and brown also work well. There are scores of other lures that work in the parks, and part of the fun is experimenting with new ones. But there is one more essential ingredient to consider before the formula for success is attained.

Line

As important as "swimming the lure" is the weight of the line used when trouting the parks. The clearer and lower the water, the greater the need for two-pound test monofilament. And to go a step further, choose a green or brown line over silver or fluorescent one. These shades further disguise your offering when the lake has the clarity of tap water. When the spring branches are high and roily, line weight or color does not play such a vital role. But through most of the winter, fish-for-fun season, and the regular season, transparent water is the norm.

There are exceptions to this rule. Those anglers after lunkers, trout of three pounds or better, start the first hour (also the best time to catch lunkers) with six- or eight-pound test. It is not that they could not land heavy trout with lighter line. But elbow-to-elbow fishing just after the siren is not the time to play a six-pounder for twenty minutes when there are fifty other people sharing the same fifteen yards of water. In other words, if you are lunker hunting that time of the morning, you had better be ready to horse the fish in so others might get on with their sport.

For most of us, a good plan is to use a spinning reel with snap-on changeable spools—one loaded with four-pound and the other with two-pound line. Start off with four-pound during dim light and the first thirty-minute frenzy of surround sound casting. Use a slightly heavier lure than you would use with two-pound test. There is a vast difference in using these two lines, and you will find the fishing less frustrating if you choose the heavier mono for starters. Most important, you can play and land your fish quickly, with less likelihood of your line becoming hopelessly tangled with those of your neighbors.

Remember also that two-pound line is more temperamental. It is more likely to kink, coil, and exhibit bad behavior during the heat of battle. Dim-light bird's nest tangles are especially miserable when everybody around you has fish on. And, if you do not have your drag set just right, and you are not using a high-quality, fresh monofilament, trout have a tendency to quickly part ways with two-pound test.

Switch to the lighter line when the sky brightens and the crowd thins. This is the time when two-pound test is a must. It enables you to cast smaller, lighter lures easily. Your offering descends more naturally, and you will catch more fish.

Fishing with Kids

It is 1948 or 1949, and a young boy in love with fishing is about to be introduced to his first boat. The boy's father steers a black 1947 Plymouth down the narrow asphalt road that leads to Greenwood Lake. It is a cool, damp June morning. The air smells fishy.

The man and boy rent a small, weathered, wooden rowboat at a place called the Bait House. It's a simple clapboard shack surrounded by aged slips that cradle rowboats that have lost most of their bright blue paint. Half the boats are already gone, rented for the morning or day by predawn fishermen bent on catching the lake's bass and hefty bluegill by surprise.

The boy learned to fish at this lake, standing on the banks of a long, narrow peninsula that jutted into clear blue water. The finger of land was stitched with several rickety docks in varying states of decay. Snubbed to some of the piers was an assortment of forgotten rowboats, some usable, it seemed, others betrayed by withered caulk, partly filled with and rotted by water. The boy fished mostly for sunfish from the tipsy docks. But with fishing came dreaming and fantasies of being in one of those boats, high and dry, casting to bass and bluegill at the edge of the lily pads at the south end of the lake.

Sometimes he carefully stepped into one of the old, tilted boats along the dock. He sat on a splintered bench seat, sometimes casting and pretending the skiff was his. It all seemed so magical, from the smell of the boat's wood to the horseshoe shape of the oarlocks. But in a young boy's mind, it was all so out of reach, until the day he and his father rented a dream come true.

They took turns rowing to the south end of the lake. When it was his turn, the boy made little headway, but it did not matter. The power of oars, the slice of blades cutting into water—hearing the creak of the old boat as it glided under the highway bridge and seeing the south end of the lake at water level was a thrill. The boat was a miracle. The boat meant freedom. And fishing, for a boy and his dad, took on new meaning.

They caught some small bass and let them go. They did keep some fat bluegill for supper. The boy, and probably the man as well, also knew that sitting in the boat together, in a beautiful spot, hoping and catching, forged a special bond between them that would last a lifetime. My father, who passed away in December 20, 2001, gave to me an appreciation of the beauty of the outdoors and fishing. I am grateful to this day. I passed the tradition of fishing and love of fishing boats on to my own children, now in their twenties.

Kids get hooked on fishing, boating, and the outdoors

rather easily provided an adult catalyst is part of the magical formula. I have yet to meet a youngster who, once introduced to the sport and tutored in a gentle, understanding manner, did not want to go fishing again . . . and again. Fishing is just plain good for the soul. It is a spirit and a hobby that inhabits mind and body for a lifetime. Sport fishing can keep a lot of kids straight, kids who otherwise may venture off course. But behind every youngster who wants to go fishing, there has to be a parent, relative, friend, or guardian who takes a boy or girl by the hand and says, "Let's go." Taking a child to a lake, pond, or stream has its frustrating and frantic moments as well as its beautiful ones. Some adults prefer going alone rather than risking the company of a kid. There will be days when a young companion will have you questioning your own sanity. But most trips are filled with memorable rewards.

Every year the Missouri Department of Conservation offers free fishing days. No permits are required. They provide a great opportunity to introduce kids to fishing. Check the department's website or the current booklet on fishing regulations for the dates.

By the way, kids who enjoy outdoor sports do not necessarily shun or give up traditional school sports like baseball, basketball, football, and soccer. Those sports all have their season, and their time, but fishing is a sport for a lifetime!

As a parent or guardian, you may know nothing about fishing. Visit the library or bookstores and select some general titles on how to catch freshwater fish. There are hundreds of books on the subject. Just a few will provide you with enough basic information to get started and begin making informed choices when buying tackle. Other learning tools are instructional videotapes and fishing seminars (generally sponsored by tackle manufacturers and retail outlets) presented by expert anglers.

It is the feel of hooking and fighting a fish that keeps fishermen of all ages coming back for more. Choose a pond or stream with an abundant supply of sunfish, catfish, bass, or trout that bite readily. It can be a private farm pond (where permission to fish has been obtained) or a small lake loaded with panfish. Pay lakes, ponds, or streams are heavily stocked and offer good first-time fishing possibilities. Inquire at local fish and game stations or call the Missouri Conservation Department. Department Offices or bait and tackle shops can provide tips about good spots to try.

First-time anglers are not overly impressed with whether a fish is a bass or a carp, just as long as they catch something. So exotic destinations and long boat rides are not necessities. The simpler the better. The more you can relax, the better you can convey the fun and inherent relaxation of the sport. If at some later date your pupils grow into tournament bass fishermen, that is their decision.

Kids enjoy keeping and eating the fish they catch. This is a natural part of the process. They can practice catch-and-release fishing later if they choose. For now, clean and fillet the fish, and by all means let the youngsters watch or even help in preparing their catch for the table.

Steps in Filleting (bass, carp, walleye, or crappie)

Start behind the fish's head, cutting down the backbone and then continuing along the length of the fish to the tail. Slice off the meat. Turn the fish over and repeat the process on the other side.

To remove the skin, reverse the process. Hold the tail firmly, cut into the fish right in front of the tail, slicing down to the skin, and slide the knife toward the head between the skin and flesh.

Pan Dressing (smaller fish)

Scrape the skin with a spoon or scaling tool to remove the scales. Remove the fins on the back and behind the stomach, making small cuts on both sides of them. Next, remove the head, and slit the belly and pull out the entrails.

Cook the fish while it is fresh by dipping in batter and frying. (If you're camping, you can also dip the fillets in a mixture of milk and egg—or in water, if that's all you have—and then roll them in flour or cornmeal that you have brought along in a ziplock bag.) I have found that kids who may not like the taste of frozen, store-bought fish enjoy eating their own fish. Fillet the fish so there are no bones. Fish can be served hot— either as a main course or in smaller pieces in sandwiches.

Treat every catch, regardless of size, like the "trophy" it is. Bring the camera and take pictures. Unfortunately, fishing snootiness, species discrimination, and the false notion that the only good fish is a lunker will probably come to your students with angling maturation. In the meantime, help them learn to appreciate and enjoy the entire experience.

A kid's attention span is directly proportional to the amount of action and number of fish caught. There is no need to spend long hours fishing. Plan a good, sensible outing the first time out. Do not inflict on him or her an all-day endurance test. Take plenty of breaks, and when the catching slows or stops, clean the fish, put them on ice in a cooler, and head home for a fish fry before your boy or girl is worn out. If you did your job well, you will have created a new angler who will never know when to quit fishing.

My son and daughter learned how to cast at the ages of five and six, respectively, using the short Snoopy rods and matching Zebco 202 closed-faced reels and a plastic practice plug minus the hooks. In a game they played, one of them would be the caster (angler) and the other the fish. Then they would reverse roles. This was one of their favorite games as preschoolers. I even got involved at times when they wanted a bigger "fish" to catch.

These rods were fine teaching tools, but I do not recommend them for actual fishing. They have about as much flex and sensitivity as broomsticks. Cooperative fish, ones that seem designed especially for youngsters, demand light responsive rods that telegraph bites and make hook setting easier.

A good choice is a five-to a five-and-a-half-foot light-action (action is marked near the bottom of the rod where it joins the handle) rod made of fiberglass or graphite. Adults use these same rods for trout and panfish. They are perfect for kids, and the price is right.

The spincast reel is a good choice for beginners. It has a cover over the spool, and line spins off the spool through a guidehole in the cover cone. This reel has a push button for the thumb on top of it for disengaging the line so that it coils off the spool when cast. With a forward crank of the reel handle, the spool is engaged, and line is retrieved. These reels come in small, medium, and large sizes and a wide range of quality and prices. Spincast reels are generally easier for kids to operate than open-face spinning reels, where coils of line can fall off the spool and cause tangles. Choose a small- or medium-size reel with good balance and comfort with a light rod. The position of the spincast reel is on top of the rod seat. Make sure the youngster can easily push the casting button when the reel is mounted on the rod.

Short-shanked hooks (numbers ten through twelve) are good for sunfish, while long-shanked hooks are better for catfish and crappie. Use small weights and split shot rather that large sinkers, which rob worms, minnows, grasshoppers, or crickets of their natural drift and descent appearance. When fishing in a stream, use just enough weight to keep the bait from being swept away by the current. The bait should settle near the bottom, where most of the fish congregate.

In still water it is best to use no weight at all in some cases. A float or bobber adds just enough weight to cast, and signals a biting fish as well. For kids and adults, the excitement of watching a float bobbing and disappearing under the surface represents what fishing is all about. Live bait generally produces better catching for children. Night crawlers work well, and kids often enjoy collecting them the evening before. Two easy-to-catch fish are bluegill and crappie. Worms are good bait for bluegill; for crappie, try small minnows.

With the right gear, kids can learn to cast lures and catch fish with them. Small lures, one-eighth ounce or lighter, are suited to light rods. Try small silver or gold-bladed in-line small crankbaits, weedless deadheaded jigs and two- to four-inch floating minnow imitations. No special action is needed to work these lures correctly, and fish generally hook themselves. Kids may not be strong enough to provide the hook-setting power necessary to use plastic worms effectively for bass. And some lures and the rods needed to cast them are just too heavy for kids to handle.

A small plastic single- or double-tray tackle box is just the right size. The box can be filled with an assortment of lures, hooks, weights, and bobbers. A pair of nail clippers with cord lanyard is handy for snipping monofilament fishing line. A nylon cord fish stringer is easy to carry and ready when needed to carry and display the catch, as well as handy for keeping fish alive in the water until you are ready to transport them home. Needle-nose pliers are useful for extracting hooks. Start kids fishing on the bank of a pond, lake, or stream. The initial teaching process is easier on solid ground. As kids become comfortable with casting lures and playing fish, the option of using a boat is part of the natural progression. This doubles the adventure for kids and adults alike. It also increases the odds of catching fish on large ponds and lakes. (Remember a well-fitting life jacket for a child fishing in deep or fast-moving water.) Boating safety and ethics goes hand in hand with fishing ethics. There is no better combination than fishing and boating for a lifetime sport. I have found that people who were introduced to fishing as children stay with it most of their lives. My daughter, Brittany, and son, Scott, now in their twenties, still fish. The sister is not as avid as her brother, but on trips she is a trooper for a while in catching slab bluegill.

Scott and I still fish together, and we also like to go fishing with our pal Curt Merz, a fine angler and former football player for the Kansas City Chiefs. He now resides in Springfield, Missouri. Curt and I teamed up for a radio program in Springfield several years ago that was centered around fishing, hunting, canoeing, camping, and specialized fishing boats. The credo is a good boat gets the lunkers.

Fishing with Curt Merz

My friend Curt wanted to fish for muskie in Lake Pomme de Terre. He had never fished for the toothy fish whose reputation is mostly known in the northeastern states. Fishermen began catching legal-sized muskellunge in Pomme de Terre Reservoir in 1968, and the establishment of a significant fishery through continuous stocking seems assured. The majority of fishermen interviewed would prefer to catch muskies over any other fish species in this reservoir; however, muskies are not expected to achieve the abundance of other game fishes and will remain "trophy" or "bonus" fish.

My introduction to muskie fishing on Pomme de Terre was a good one. I was fishing with Bob Hippie, of Long Lane, Missouri. Hippie had become addicted to the sport and wanted to show me how he got involved with this habit-forming fish officially known as muskellunge (*Esox masquinongy*). We fished all day without a strike, and I was beginning to believe that our quarry was a ghost fish. We had thrown big baits—such as Bobbie baits, Teddie's Big Jerk, Suick, Killer Bucktail and Jointed Pikie—until our arms and shoulders ached, but nothing was biting. We stopped for a midafternoon nap on the shore of the sandy swimming beach. We both conked out quickly. When we woke up an hour later, it was time to head out again. Bob told me that late afternoon until sunset was the prime time.

Four hours later the sun was setting over the hills. I had just hung a yellow bucktail solidly in a stump, and frustration had set in, when all hell broke loose. The fish leaped completely out of the water and hung suspended for a moment before crashing wildly back into the water. Hippie had the monster tethered. His stout rod was bowed nearly in two, and I would have bet on the muskie at that point.

I ran for the oversized net and jammed it in the water. Bob, a veteran of the muskie wars, kept the fish's head up and guided him quickly into the mesh. A thirty-five-inch, twelve-pound trophy was admired, quickly photographed, and released. After signing the release, which entitles the

Scott Farmer and Curt Merz fishing at Table Rock Lake

angler to a certificate and a patch from the Conservation Department, Bob and I headed home exhausted. While I did not get a strike that day, my partner's dramatic catch made me a believer in the power of *Esox*. I vowed to return to Pomme and try my luck again.

I have made six trips to Pomme de Terre since then in the company of my fishing partner, Curt Merz, who is more addicted to muskie fishing than I am. To date, neither Curt nor I have been successful. We have not even had a strike, despite fishing with our friend "Muskie Bill" Mueller, who has tangled with *Esox* often and is considered one of the best guides on the lake. Bill has gotten to the point where he

Scott Farmer and Curt Merz show off their catch, bass from Table Rock Lake

feels sorry for us. Our wives pity us. They cannot understand our annual pilgrimages to the lake. They call *Esox* a mythical denizen and say that we are gluttons for punishment. "Why don't you fish for normal fish like everybody else?" They scoff!

According to the pamphlet "Muskies in Missouri," published by the Missouri Department of Conservation, on many northern lakes, it may take sixty to one hundred hours to catch a legal (thirty inches or more) muskie. On Lake Pomme de Terre it may take only twenty to twenty-five hours to catch a legal fish. Curt and I have proven the Missouri statistics wrong, and we are closing in on those used for northern lakes. We have over fifty hours invested in on-water casting. It is still enjoyable, of course, and one of these days our efforts will finally pay off. The fishing forecast published by the MDC says the muskie fishing should be excellent because legal fish are abundant due to stockings in 1984 and 1989-1991. The report says that muskies in the thirty-six to forty inch range are fairly common. Catch-and-release fishing for sublegal muskies will also be good due to the 1992 stocking of 6,615 fish. Best angling occurs between September 15 and October 15 at water temperatures near seventy degrees Farenheit.

Fishing Lake Taneycomo

In the early hours of October 29, 1987, when most fishermen were in bed, Dave Bethurem of Springfield, was plying the frigid waters of Lake Taneycomo. Between midnight and sunrise, fishing a 1/100-ounce black marabou jig on his seven-foot graphite fly rod, he caught two rainbow trout—one weighing thirteen pounds, eight ounces, and one weighing and nine pounds, fourteen ounces. He caught the fish at the head of a fast-water shoot that, according to Bethurem, "looked two feet deep, but is really only five foot deep."

Most anglers would have headed home after landing two trophies, but hunting big trout is an addiction, and the Ozarks angler knew there are few places in the nation better than Taneycomo for lunker prospecting. Close to 8 a.m., with several fishermen now sharing the same pool, the skilled fly-rodder, Bethurem, added two more rainbows of seven and four pounds, respectively. Like most of the fish he catches, the trout were quickly and safely released. When Bethurem is on a roll, his fishing days crowd together.

About twenty minutes before sunrise the next day, a heavy fish inhaled his number six wooly bugger. He was fishing Taneycomo's "Brown Hole" with his friend Mark Gooding when the strike occurred. Bethurem knew it was a big brown.

He thought during the forty-minute struggle he might even have a new record tethered to his four-pound tippet. The trout cut through the big hole for about 250 yards before Dave could slow the fish. It had taken all of Bethurem's fly line, plus about fifty yards of backing. It was well after daylight when Dave landed the fish. The hook-jawed brown trout was brilliantly marked in full spawning coloration and still looked like a record-breaker. The fish was weighed on commercial food scales at Steel's Bait and Tackle a short drive from the dam. The fat female weighed fourteen pounds, two ounces. The state record at the time was fifteen pounds, eleven ounces for brown trout.

The Conservation Department keeps a list of Missouri State Record Fish and the anglers who catch them. If you think you have a record-breaking fish, keep in mind these rules to get your catch recognized by the Department of Conservation:

The fish must be weighed in the presence of a Conservation Department employee.

A Conservation Department fisheries biologist must make an official identification of the fish.

Dave Bethurem's success is just one example of what awaits anglers at Taneycomo. The lake is, without a doubt, one of the most easily accessed trophy trout waters in the nation. Some of the best fishing is just below the dam, near the Missouri Department of Conservation Shepherd of the Hills Fish Hatchery. The points where the hatchery outlet streams enter the lake are extremely popular spots.

As is true in the trout parks, there are hundreds of different ways to fish the frigid waters of Taneycomo. Bank fishermen and waders, using spinning gear or fly rods, use lures, flies and live bait. The same lures used at the trout parks are effective at the lake. Silver Little Cleo spoons are also top producers. Wooly buggers and scud imitations are

Jeannie Muller at Lake Taneycomo—fine fishing on a cold day

excellent fly patterns along with a variety of weighted nymphs. When it comes to bait, Taneycomo trout are not finicky. Night crawlers, miniature marshmallows, kernel corn, prepared Power Bait, salmon eggs, cheese balls, and wax worms entice their share of fish. Boat anglers have access to a varied number of good spots for catching, drifting, or trolling with live baits and the lures mentioned. Special caution should be used when water is being released through the dam.

Here are some important tips. Some of the best fishing at Taneycomo is during the winter. Some of the best fishing is at night, if you can stand the cold. There are anglers who use nothing but 1/32-ounce brown marabou jigs when fishing the lake. With ultralight rod and reel equipped with two-pound test line, they use the "jigs-swim" method to catch one trout after another. It's all in the touch.

In recent years, due to unbridled development in the Branson area, the water quality in Lake Taneycomo has declined. Most veteran anglers believe the catching of big fish is not as good as it once was. Despite the negative impact of the building boom on the lake, the trout fishing in Taneycomo is still better than average, and anglers still have a good chance of catching a lunker. Hopefully, tougher water-quality regulations will be implemented to protect water quality in the lake. Taneycomo is too great a fishing treasure to let die!

The Game Fish of Missouri:
How to Find Them and Catch Them

The Missouri Department of Conservation has a fine publication on game fish found in the state that will help both new anglers and seasoned fishermen. The pamphlet's color photos make it easy to identify the freshwater fishes that are most popular, which include the following: The largemouth bass is one of the most popular. The smallmouth bass also ranks high. Other fish include white crappie, bluegill, channel catfish, rock bass, white bass, flathead catfish, black bullhead, white bass-striped bass hybrid, rainbow trout, walleye, and muskellunge.

Hunting

I never really knew if Dad liked to get up at 4 a.m. on a Saturday and drive two hours to the property of a farmer friend of ours who was gracious enough to let us hunt quail and cottontail rabbits on his land near Osceola, Missouri.

The night before our hunt, I could never get to sleep—too much thinking about quail, cottontails, and Farmer Bill's bird dog, Max, who made our hunt easy most of the time. Max could smell out a covey of bobwhites like no other bird dog. Pure dog work in progress. At times, Bill lent Max to us.

All these thoughts in the middle of the night kept me awake. Dad, however, snored like a trooper who had not had a decent sleep in months. On workdays, Dad would jump out of bed, shave, eat, and get ready for the workweek, but hunting days, he was in slow motion. Most times, we actually got up together. I would whisper in Dad's ear, "We need to get our clothes on and pack our gear for the hunt." I assured him that the three clocks in the house were all running the same. It took him about twenty minutes to get dressed. Saturdays were not days for shaving. Facial stubble was my dad's best friend during the hunting season. He liked the ruggedness for hunting quail.

We both had mustard-colored hunting coats and pants, which were made to take a beating. Game bags were sewn into the coats. Large pockets held shotgun shells. The coats and pants were not only durable; good brands were also waterproof. Our leather hunting boots could stand up to

Author quail hunting in Missouri

rain, snow, and mud. Mustard-colored caps, also sturdy and waterproof, were made with earflaps that kept the warmth in on cold, wet days. Woolen socks kept our feet warm, and woolen mittens or gloves, part of the hunters' garb, kept our hands warm.

Food played a big part in the hunt. Mom always made sure that Dad and I had meat sandwiches, cookies, and hot drinks in Thermos bottles (coffee for Dad, hot chocolate for me). We went walking along in hopes that a covey of quail scented by Max was just around the cornfield or in the brush.

Sometimes, the birds were not to be seen, so we'd break

Quail hunters with dog

for lunch. Dad and I would find a large downed tree made perfect for a table. Then we'd settle down for lunch. This part of the hunt was always a time for bonding and was filled with great conversation. Dad would speak great words of wisdom saying, "It seems every time we eat our lunch, the birds seem to open up." We'd laugh. I guess Mom's good cooking had something to do with it. Being famished, we devoured our food. Max would watch us; his anxious eyes, wagging tail, and slobbery mouth let me know he was hungry, so I reached into my coat pocket and pulled out some dog biscuits. I gave him a pat, and he licked my face as if to say, "Thank you!" We

Pointer on quail hunt

knew the birds would work for us and Max. Hunting quail and rabbits is a good thing.

After a short siesta, we ready our shotguns for the afternoon hunt. It's a cool day for hunting. The quail should be fortified with grain in the corn rows. Max is in prime condition. Suddenly, he is on point on a stubble patch. We are about twenty yards from the dog. Slowly we head toward Max. In an instant, a whisper of birds flies up for a getaway. Dad and I use Remington autoloading shotguns with three-shot capacity. We are ready when the bobwhites sail over our heads. Dad drops two birds, and I power a single. With Max's amazing scent he easily finds the birds. We put the quail in our game bags.

We thought that the birds that had vanished were long gone. Once again, Max was ahead of us. We could not see him in the shallow ravine not far from us. Dad whispered softly, "Looks to me like Max has some more birds. Maybe some of those birds are still around." Sure enough, Max was on point again. We had a good spot to shoot. This time, I would get first pickin's. It turned out to be the best shooting ever. I got four birds with three shots. Dad was so happy that he jumped up and down like a pup.

Maybe the best thing that day was making sure we had the Brownie camera. Dad snapped a shot of me holding the bobwhite quail. Then I snapped a shot of Dad, grinning from ear to ear, holding his birds. We didn't forget Max. After all, he was really the hero. Yes, lots of dog biscuits and plenty of snapshots too of our friend, Max. We bought Farmer Bill and his wife, Mary, a nice big juicy ham for their Sunday meal to thank our good friends on the farm for giving us the privilege of hunting.

Understanding Hunting Goes a Long Way

In an age dominated more and more by urban and suburban values, a significant share of Americans have little understanding of modern sport hunting or the reasons why men and women hunt. Missouri, and the Ozarks in particular, remains a stronghold of hunting tradition and ties with nature and the land. The Springfield–Upper White River region, which was once prime hunting land for the Osage Indian tribe, is being chewed up by commercial and residential development. As trees are bulldozed, hills leveled, streams degraded, and topsoil paved over, city ethics and attitudes displace the rural love and respect for green space and the natural order.

The transition has a negative effect on every living creature and is especially damaging to fish and wildlife as well as to the anglers, hunters, and trappers who pursue them. "Gentle-men farmers' estates" and newly developed housing plots stretch into prime hunting and fishing areas, causing conflicts between outdoors enthusiasts and residents seeking the "rural life" complete with all the latest conveniences. In most cases, modern bow and gun hunters get the short end of the stick.

Aldo Leopold, noted conservationist and author of *A Sand County Almanac* said, "We of the industrial age boast of our control over nature. Plant or animal, star or atom, wind or rivers—there is no foreseen Earth or sky which will not shortly harness to build 'the good life for ourselves.'"

Unfortunately, the region's siege of wilderness cannot be stopped. Trite and overused—"money wins out in the end" is a sure bet. In addition to the problem of habitat destruction, in the past decade, hunters across the nation, who help reduce animal populations, have taken it on the chin from antihunters and animals rights activists who feel that wild animals and birds, big and small, should be spared from effective and scientifically regulated hunting seasons.

Ironically, it is not until wild deer, turkeys, rabbits, raccoons, squirrels, coyotes, beavers, and other critters start munching on crops, livestock, gardens, flowers, shrubs, nursery trees, insulation, and pets that the animal activists learn what hunters have always known. In a society that sacrifices its best wildlife habitat for shopping malls and condos, today's balance of nature works only when there is a controlled and scientifically proven harvest of game animals, game birds, and furbearers.

Hunters and trappers carry out the mission of modern game management in the most effective way possible. Over the last fifty years, numbers of wild animals have increased or stabilized in the nation as a whole as well as in Missouri, resulting in healthy herds, flocks, coveys, and packs. Yet, there is an antihunting sentiment out there that regularly surfaces at workplaces, social gatherings, schools, and churches when the topic of hunting crops up.

Hunters, hunting organizations, and fish and game departments like the Missouri Department of Conservation are coming out with modern game and fish management, and it's working. Hunters and anglers generate most of the money for wildlife conservation.

All fifty states now have laws on the books that prevent hunters from being harassed by those opposed to sport hunting. Missouri law states, "It shall be considered a violation of any person who intentionally harasses, drives or disturbs game animals for the purpose of disrupting lawful hunting or trapping in the first degree."

In Missouri, if hunters are harassed on Conservation Department lands, they should contact a conservation agent. If they are harassed on private lands, they should contact the sheriff's office or police department. It goes without saying that permission from the landowner is required when hunting on private land. Hunters in Missouri regard hunting as a deep-rooted tradition and a greatly appreciated privilege.

New Turkeys in Missouri Forests Means Good Hunting in Fall

When the pioneers arrived in territory that would later be called Missouri with their wagons, horses, and other possessions, the land held plenty of game, including rabbit, deer, turkey, waterfowl, doves, snipe, woodcock, and rails, and there were fish in the clear rivers and streams. As the procession of pioneers settled in Missouri, more and more wild turkeys were on the menu. The birds were easy to dress out for eating. Venison was also good, but nothing was better than wild turkey.

It is hard to believe that by 1806 turkeys were getting scarce in Missouri. From the 1920s clear up into the 1970s, turkeys were hard to find. It was then that the Missouri Department of Conservation and its wildlife research biologists began to try to remedy Missouri's wild turkey shortage. The problem? Too many birds harvested between 1806 and the 1970s.

Scott Farmer turkey hunting

Since the Conservation Department took action, hunting has improved. Turkeys in Missouri are holding their own thanks to the Missouri Department of Conservation and the wildlife research biologists that care for wildlife and Missouri hunters! Hunters can go after turkey during seasons in both the spring and the fall. Hunting regulations for turkeys consist of seasons, methods, and limits. Spring season annually will begin on the Monday closest to April 21. All hunters must have the prescribed turkey hunting permit and may take turkeys according to the season length and bag limit

Scott Farmer after successful turkey hunt

established annually by the Conservation Commission.

Fall firearms season annually begins on the second Monday in October and is fourteen days in length. A person possessing the prescribed turkey hunting permit may take two turkeys of either sex during the season, provided that only one turkey is taken per day. The Missouri Department of Conservation has fall firearms permits for turkey hunting running October 13 to October 26.

The department publishes pamphlets on turkey hunting each year, which are available either from the department or

Author turkey hunting near Table Rock Lake

from the various check stations. Hunters can also pick up a copy of the *Wildlife Code of Missouri: Rules of the Conservation Commission.*

Areas good for hunting wildlife are in the Mark Twain Forest Wilderness, which encompasses Piney Creek, Hercules Glades, Paddy Creek, Irish Wilderness, Bell Mountain Wilderness, Rockpile Wilderness, and Devil's Backbone Wilderness.

Mingo Wilderness is managed by the U.S. Fish and Wildlife Service and Forest Service. For more information, send your request to the following address:

Jeannie Muller turkey hunting, Mark Twain National Forest

Mark Twain National Supervisor's Office, 401 Fairgrounds Road, Rolla, MO 65401 Phone: (573-364-4621).

Some of the finest turkey hunting is in October. The beauty of the cool mornings, shortleaf pines, wild turkeys, and squirrels make for enjoyable hunting.

Dogwoods in the fall and winter are good for deer and wild turkeys and provide gray squirrels' habitat. Sugar maple leaves turn brilliant reds and yellows. The shortleaf pine in Missouri is good habitat for turkeys, deer, rabbits, doves, snipe, and woodcock.

Women on Target—from the Women of the NRA

The National Rifle Association's Women on Target program began in 1999 and continues to offer three effective ways for women to enter or advance in the hunting or shooting sports: women-only hunting excursions, charity shoots, and instructional shooting clinics that allow beginners to have safe and enjoyable first-time experiences with firearms. Women who already have a hunting or shooting background will find unprecedented camaraderie and a chance to mentor other women with the same interest in the outdoors. More than one hundred instructional shooting clinics are anticipated. Call or visit the NRA website for a current schedule.

For a Women on Target press kit, or for help in attending one of these events, call, (703) 267-1595 or go to www.nrahq.org/womenfindex.asp.

Women on Target Charity Shoot schedules are located in Branson, Missouri; Houston, Texas; and Guthrie, Oklahoma.

The hunting area includes pronghorn antelope in Glenrock, Wyoming; mallard duck in Queenstown, Maryland; pheasant/chukar in Brainard, Nebraska; dove in Coalinga, California; white deer in Havelock, North Carolina; mule deer in Vaughn, New Mexico; whitetail deer/boar in Fairhope, Pennsylvania; and white deer in Mountain Home, Texas.

Poling for Ducks

Unless you have done it since you were eight years old, poling a flat-bottom plywood duck boat into the teeth of a twenty-knot northwest November wind before daylight is a bad dream that never seems to end. My good friend Ed Weissler and I found ourselves in such a predicament at Grand Pass Wildlife Management Area seven miles west of Marshall. Ed put it best. "If anybody had been watching us from the bank, they would have thought we had gone mad." It would have been funny at the time if we had not been desperately trying to reach our shooting pool by legal light. We could hear and see hundreds of ducks overhead. Our hosts, who were leading the way, poled straight and strong, all the while calling back encouragement.

"You'll get the hang of it," they shouted over the wind. "Take your time."

After twenty minutes of fighting the wind, a fifteen-foot pole with a metal "duck bill" snubber on one end, and a boat that simply would not go where I wanted, I jumped out and pulled the boat through the marsh. Rarely do I give up on anything. Fortunately, I had chest waders on, and the water was only knee deep. An hour earlier, waterfowl biologist Dale Humburg had suggested that I didn't have to wear waders at all. "We do everything from the boats," he said. "There's no reason to get out of the boat, and everything stays nice and dry."

If I'd heeded Humburg's advice, I thought later, I would have spent the entire day poling in circles three feet forward, six feet backward capped off by 180-degree windblown windmill turns that always left me headed in the wrong direction. This had all started after the drawing that determined whether we would hunt pool three or pool four.

"By the way," Dale asked casually, "have you ever poled a boat?" "Once," I told him, "I tried poling my canoe up the Finley River." He grinned but never asked me if I was successful at standing up in a seventeen-foot canoe, snubbing my way upstream. I didn't tell him how much water I took into my lungs that day.

The waterfowl biologist, I found out later, had been poling duck boats since childhood. First in Iowa, then in Missouri. A twinge of anxiety struck Ed and me when Humburg proclaimed, "Well, you'll be poling your own boats today. It really adds a nice quality to shallow-water hunting, and it's perfect for Grand Pass."

Then, all of sudden, we were out there in the blackness. I finally bailed out, soaked with perspiration under layers of wool and Gore-Tex. Despite plodding through oozing mud and foot-trapping vegetation, it felt better to walk. I was making progress. Ed was not faring too well either, so Dale sped back and tied their boats together. He towed Ed to the shooting pool with long, smooth strokes and some deft back-pole ruddering. George and Mike, our other partners, had most of the ninety decoys out by the time I slogged into the shooting pool, I felt like a greenhorn leading a spirited horse to the barn rather than riding it. I was the novice skier taking the tram down the mountain with skis still in hand. But I was there, and I was dry, and ducks were milling around everywhere.

Duck hunters, Four Rivers

After the decoys were set, we snugged the five boats together (three of them handmade by Dale) and camouflaged their decks with woven marsh grass mats. Mike's yellow lab, Charlie, sat between two of the boats on a brown plastic milk crate. With boat cushions under our rumps and behind our backs, we lay comfortably in the low-profile blinds, out of the wind, dry, shotguns resting on our chests. From that point, until we quit at eleven-thirty, the longest break in the action was perhaps five minutes. A bullish front had whipped in from the northwest during the night. The nearly thirty thousand ducks using Grand Pass for food were restless for the first time in two weeks. Our timing could not have been better.

Dale and George worked their calling together nicely. The decoys bobbed briskly, and for the first hour, flocks of mallards, pintails, and green-winged teal came in cupped and seemingly suspended in front of us. Our biggest obstacle was politeness. Nobody wanted to shoot first, or perhaps no one wanted to miss such "easy" shots. From our view at near water level. I was mesmerized by the show of wings. Finally, after we had let four or five flocks slip away with all feathers intact, the guns starting booming, and drake greenheads fell. The retriever was fulfilling his primary role in life. Suddenly I felt part of the pole boat and the marsh. After thirty years of duck hunting, I was discovering a new phase of the sport, and its pleasure was oozing into my veins.

The mallard flights stopped midmorning, for some reason, and bunches of wary pintails took up the slack. Ever cautious, they were more difficult to lure into gun range. "Just like pintails," Dale chided, as the birds that were seemingly hooked flew just out of range. Enough of them came in to enable each of us to add a sprig to our bag. Dale spotted a black duck, uncommon in the Mississippi flyway, that slipped in and out of range quickly. The biologist, I'm convinced, is part duck himself, although he has eyes like a hawk.

Too soon the shoot was over. With the wind at our backs this time, Ed and I poled the distance back to the ramp. Grand Pass is a wetland treasure restored. I will be back, and chances are good that I will be poling my own boat.

Every Duck Hunter I Know Wants to Shoot a Wood Duck

My duck-hunting dad told me that he wanted in the worst way to shoot a wood duck. It took him two years to knock down a woody. He did not want to eat the beautiful male. Instead, he took the bird to a taxidermist. To many duck hunters, the woody drake is the best of all.

The wood duck is the common duck of open woodland around lakes and along streams. The large head, short neck, and long square tail are good field marks. No other duck has the long slicked-back crest. The dull-colored female has a white eye ring. Males in eclipse, or colored, plumage resemble the female but are whiter under the chin. Their flight is rapid; wood ducks dodge gracefully between the trees. They feed on plant materials, such as duckweed and acorns, which they crush in their gizzards, and various kinds of insects. They nest in natural tree cavities and nest boxes. Their call is a distinctive rising whistle.

Puddle ducks can be found in shallow marshes and rivers rather than in large lakes and bays. They are good divers. Most feed by dabbling or tipping rather than by submerging. Puddle ducks feed in croplands. They walk and run well on land. Their diet consists mostly of vegetables. Grain-fed mallards, pintails, or acorn-fattened wood ducks are highly regarded as food for the hunter. All of them can take flight almost instantly by jumping straight into the air, from land or water.

Diving ducks frequent the larger, deeper lakes and rivers as well as coastal bays and inlets. The colored wing patches of these birds lack the brilliance of the speulums of puddle ducks. Since many of them have short tails, their huge paddle feet may be used as rudders in flight. Most of these groups paddle along the water before becoming airborne.

As their name suggests, they feed by diving, often to considerable depths. To escape danger, they can travel great distances underwater, emerging only enough to show their heads before submerging again. Their diets of fish, shellfish, mollusks, and aquatic plants make them second choice, as a group, for sportsmen. Canvasbacks and redheads fattened on eel grass and wild celery are notable exceptions. Since their wings are smaller in proportion to the size and weight of their bodies they have a more rapid wingbeat than puddle ducks.

The greater white-fronted goose is a grayish brown goose with a white band between the face and bill. The bill is normally pink with a white tip. Its brown belly is heavily marked with black barbs and spotting. It migrates generally in the central and Pacific flyways and is also present in the Mississippi flyway but is rare to the Atlantic flyway.

The lesser white-fronted goose has a white blaze and black belly patches in adult plumage. It has a bright yellow eye ring and a white forehead with a pinkish-orange bill. It is mainly found in the central and Pacific flyways and is also present in the Mississippi flyway but is rarely found in the Atlantic flyway.

Snow geese have two phases. White-phase geese are

Scott Farmer after successful goose hunt, Four Rivers

white all over with distinctive black wing tips. Blue-phase birds have white heads and necks, contrasting with largely brown bodies. Both phases have pink bills with a characteristic black lip line. Greater snow geese are found along the Atlantic Coast, and lesser snow geese are found elsewhere on the continent.

Ross's geese are smaller and similar to snow geese. Most are white bodied with black wing tips, but rarely a blue-phase goose occurs. Its bill is pinkish with black marks at the base. The bill lacks the black lip line found in the snow goose.

Generally, Ross's geese are found in the central flyway, particularly in eastern New Mexico, Nebraska, Texas, and Oklahoma.

Canada geese have black necks and heads with white chin straps and black bills. Below the neck, their feathers are dusky brown with dark brown bottoms. Canada geese are found all over the United States, ranging from the Atlantic to the Pacific Coast and from Mexico north to the Arctic Coast of Canada.

Giant Canada geese are large geese with light gray breasts; black necks, black on the fronts of the heads, white cheek patches and white spots on the backs of the heads. They are found mainly in the Mississippi and central flyways.

During migration, geese may form enormous flocks numbering in the ten thousands. Each flock flies in a V-formation or in long undulating lines behind a leader. Geese fly with deep, powerful wingbeats that carry them hundreds of thousands of miles between wintering grounds and breeding grounds. Migrating geese usually fly at forty to sixty miles per hour, and some travel at tremendous heights.

Field Dressing Birds

Field dressing upland birds and waterfowl is essentially the same as field dressing other animals. The hunter's goal is to remove the entrails promptly after the bird is harvested with a minimum of mess.

Begin by plucking off the bird's belly feathers. Make a single incision at the anus and circle it with the knife, then cut up to the breastbone. Carefully insert two fingers far up into the body cavity and gently pull free the stomach and intestine. Finally pull free the lower intestine and the anus.

Drain the body cavity and store it in a cool, well-ventilated area. Let the carcass cool for a short time, then place it in a ziplock bag with a label of what species is in the bag. Chill with ice or place in a freezer. Remember, as a hunter, you should take care of good game meat for the table!

Scott Farmer duck hunting, Four Rivers

Ducks Unlimited

Ducks Unlimited (DU) was founded more than sixty-five years ago, during the Dust Bowl years of the 1930s, when a group of sportsmen banded together. North America's drought plagued waterfowl, and populations plunged to unprecedented lows. The founders of DU decided to do something about it. They incorporated the Fledgling Conservation Group in 1937, and within a year 6,720 supporters had raised $90,000.

Ducks Unlimited is the world's largest private waterfowl and wetlands conservation organization with more than 699,000 members. The organization sponsors projects throughout the United States, Canada, Mexico, the Caribbean, and Latin America. Missouri Ducks Unlimited chapters are some of the best in the nation.

In 1970, 50,000 to 281,600 duck hunters statewide harvested 149,300 mallards. In 1980, 39,300 hunters harvested 123,500 mallards. In 1990, 23,100 hunters harvested 62,600 mallards, and in the year 2000, 31,987 hunters harvested 216,500 mallards.

Successful duck hunters and Labrador retriever

Retrievers

A good retriever is the duck hunter's best friend. There are several good breeds. The Chesapeake Bay retriever is a very sturdy dog, great with waterfowl but can be a bit strong-willed. The flat-coated American water spaniel, the Irish water spaniel, and the standard poodle all have their admirers. The golden retriever is very popular, a good water dog, and both smart and quick. But the best retriever, without a doubt, is the Labrador retriever. Labs are large, strong, quick, alert, good-natured, eager to please (making them easily trained), and they have an excellent sense of smell. Besides being a fine gun dog, a Labrador makes a great family pet. According to the American Kennel Club, the Labrador is the most popular dog in America.

The Labrador originated in Newfoundland, where it was trained to bring fishing nets through icy waters. In the nineteenth century the Newfoundland fishermen traveled to the English West Country to sell fish. Some were persuaded to sell their dogs too. The breed was immediately successful in England as a gun dog. Labradors were used in both world wars to detect mines. Their present-day duties include working as police dogs and sniffing out drugs. The dog has a history of solid breeding, good training, and years of service. You won't find a better dog or a more agreeable hunting companion.

The Boone and Crockett Club

The Boone and Crockett Club was and continues to be in the forefront of the wildlife conservation movement in the United States. The club was founded in 1887 by Theodore Roosevelt and several friends who recognized the importance of saving wildlife on an area in Wyoming called Yellowstone. They realized that Americans were losing our most valuable resources: wildlife and natural habitat. These visionaries witnessed the consequences of the unrestricted killing of wildlife, pioneer settlement, and Native American government.

Under the leadership of men such as Roosevelt, Aldo Leopold, and J. N. (Ding) Darling, these club members sought protection for our natural resources with the passage of laws and the designation of wild lands. Our national forests, national parks, and national wildlife refuges exist today because of the efforts of these individuals. Records kept by the Boone and Crockett Club were essential to these efforts. During the 1920s, in response to public interest in big game, the club recognized the need for an official measurement and scoring system to record trophy animals. The

Boone and Crockett Club's method proved to also be an effective method of assessing the success of the new conservation policies.

Currently, every three years, top-scoring entries in each category are invited for the final awards judging public display of trophies and awards banquet. Only those trophies that are remeasured by the judges' panel are eligible to receive awards. Place awards are reserved for Fair Chase trophies entered by hunters. Other invited trophies, such as trophies that are found or of unknown origin, are eligible only for certificates of merit. Since the first publication of the club's *Records of North American Big Game* in 1932, there has been an emphasis on understanding species biology and habitat management to ensure the future of all species.

The Pope & Young Club

The Pope & Young Club is one of North America's leading bowhunting and conservation organizations. Founded in 1961 as a nonprofit scientific organization, the club is patterned after the prestigious Boone and Crockett Club. The club advocates and encourages responsible bowhunting by promoting quality, fair chase hunting, and sound conservation practices. Today it fosters and nourishes bowhunting excellence and acts in the best heritage everywhere. The club promotes and participates in improving sound wildlife conservation practices and wise use of natural resources.

Named in honor of pioneer bowhunters Gaston Pope and Arthur Young, whose exploits during the early part of the twentieth century drew national attention to this "forgotten" and challenging form of hunting, the Pope & Young Club began in 1957 as a part of the National Field Archery Association's Hunting Activities Committee out of a need to improve the image of bowhunting. Through its records program, the club encourages quality bowhunting by awakening interest in outstanding examples of this continent's big game animals. The club records for posterity scientific data on North American big game taken with bow and arrow.

It conducts ongoing recording periods, and every two years it recognizes the finest specimens and the hunters who submitted them. These biennial presentations honor the quality of Individual examples of the various North American big game species and promote the ideals of fair chase. Through the club's conservation program, members lead others to participate in protecting and promoting wildlife, wildlife conservation, and our bowhunting outdoors heritage.

Rules of Fair Chase Bow and Arrow (from the Pope & Young Club)

The term *fair chase* shall not include the taking of animals under the following conditions:
1. Helpless in a trap, deep snow or water, or on ice.
2. From any power vehicle or power boat.
3. While confined behind fences as on game farms, etc.
4. By "jacklighting" or shining at night.
5. By the use of any tranquilizers or poisons.
6. By the use of any power vehicles for herding or driving animals, including use of aircraft to land alongside or to communicate with or direct a hunter on the ground.
7. By the use of electronic devices for attracting, locating or pursuing game, or guiding the hunter to such game, or by the use of a bow or arrow to which any electronic device is attached.
8. Any other condition considered by the Board of Directors as unsportsmanlike.

Sora, Virginia Rails, Common Snipe, American Woodcock

Sora, nine inches from tip of the beak to tip of tail, are common migrants that forage in marshes, swamps, wet pastures, and flooded fields. Adults have short, yellow bills and black faces. Cheeks and breasts are gray with black, and bellies are white-barred. Backs are dark brown mixed with reddish tan and streaked with white. Their call is a loud, descending, nasal whinny.

Virginia rail, nine and a half inches from the tips of their beaks to the tips of their tails, forage in marshes and swamps for snails and earthworms. Adults have black backs with rusty wing patches, gray faces, and reddish bills and legs. The underparts are cinnamon with heavily barred black-and-white flanks. Their call is a series of one- and two-syllable notes, "kik, kik, kik, kidik, kidik, kidik."

Common snipe, eleven inches from the tips of their beaks to the tips of their tails, forage in marshes, swamps, wet pastures, crop stubble, and drainage ditches. They have long bills, plump bodies, and black-and-white-streaked heads. Their backs are brown and black with strong white streaks. When surprised, they take off in a zigzag pattern and call a harsh "scrape, scrape." American woodcock, or timberdoddle, are eleven inches from the tips of their beaks to the tips of their tails. They forage in young woodlands near water, moist pastures, and forested floodplains. Most common in eastern Missouri along the Mississippi lowlands, they are distinguished by extremely long bills; round, plump bodies; short tails and legs; and large black eyes. Their backs are dark and their underparts buff. When flushed, they make a starling whirring sound with their rounded, short wings.

Upland Game Birds

Ruffed grouse may be hunted from October 15 through January 15 in parts of Boone, Callaway, Montgomery, and Warren counties. Daily limit–two ruffed grouse; possession limit–four ruffed grouse.

Male pheasants may be hunted from November though January from the Kansas line to the Illinois line and those portions of DeKalb and Buchanan counties lying south of U.S. Highway 36, and all of Platte and St. Charles counties. Daily limit—two male pheasants; possession limit—four male pheasants.

Hunting quail and doves is good exercise, and the birds make fine eating. September through February is the open season for the white goose.

Camping: Still the Best for Missouri Adventure

John Muir, naturalist, brought the preservation of camping environments to the public's attention. Muir influenced President Cleveland to designate thirteen national forests. In 1903 President Theodore Roosevelt went camping with John Muir in the Yosemite forest region. Muir had a lavish approach to camping. On his campouts, he brought with him expensive hunting and fishing gear, binoculars, and fine sketch pads.

Roosevelt, a heroic conservationist, helped to establish one hundred fifty national forests, five national parks, eighteen national monuments, four national game parks, twenty-one reclamation projects, and fifty-one federal bird reservations.

Most people can't travel in the style set by John Muir, but equipment developed especially for outdoor use can make camping easier and more enjoyable. Modern campers have William C. Coleman, a salesman from Wichita, Kansas, to thank for much of the camp equipment we consider standard today. Coleman suffered from poor eyesight and was drawn to the light business. His first design was the arc lamp. Then came the first camp stove, in which Coleman used unleaded fuel for camping appliances. The 520 GI pocket stove was used by soldiers during war. The red Coleman single gas lanterns with mantles illuminated many a dark campsite. There were also green lanterns. In the boonies, a camper

Jeannie Muller backpacking, Mark Twain National Forest

could have a lot of light from one or two lanterns and still have a cheery fire with sticks and logs. A lantern would also light up a table for eating or for playing cards. The lanterns, still made today, are as tough as the great outdoors.

I have three lanterns that are still working exceptionally well—two double red lanterns and one model 2000 Liquid Fuel Lantern called the NorthStar. The NorthStar has push-button ignition—matchless lighting—and is easier to operate than one lit with a match. It operates on Coleman fuel or regular unleaded gasoline.

My Friend Sheldon Coleman and the Coleman Company

Sheldon Coleman took over the Coleman Company in 1951. He had all the credentials to make the Coleman Company as good as it had been under the founder, William C. Coleman. Sheldon was a fine fly fisherman. He fished for trout, salmon, arctic char, marlin, and other kinds of fish all over the world. Sheldon enjoyed deep-sea and freshwater fishing. He had a big heart for the outdoors and for the men and women who cherished what he loved. A savvy man who knew what outdoor people wanted when it came to tents, coolers, jugs, sleeping bags, and electric and battery-powered lights.

In 1988, Sheldon Coleman had led the company's rise for three decades and gained the respect of a nation as an outdoorsman, conservationist, and businessman. He died at the age of eighty-six. By the end of the 1980s, the Coleman Company was turning out fifteen million products a year. In the 1990s, the product expansion was robust with the addition of a comprehensive offering of camping furniture, a full line of accessories, butane-powered appliances, and innovative designs for tents and other soft goods. Coleman's X-series stoves, which run on the revolutionary Coleman Powermax fuel system, earned *Backer Magazine*'s editors' choice distinction. The fifty-millionth Coleman lantern was produced in 1995.

In 1998 Coleman was purchased by Sunbeam Corporation. In 2001, Coleman celebrated its centennial birthday. The Coleman line is still an unparalleled system of products for campers and boaters.

Innovations in Backpacking and Camping Equipment

With the advent of lighter materials like nylon, aluminum, and plastics, one could enjoy the freedom of traveling longer distances on foot. In the 1960s and '70s, this inspired legions of people to go hiking. Manufacturers responded to the backpacking craze by designing lighter, more flexible packs that fit backpackers better. Today's backpacks commonly use internal frames because they are lighter, more flexible, and fit backpackers better.

One of the first items using the lighter materials to come on the market was the Eureka draw-tight tent. It set the precedent for good tent design. In 1970 JanSport developed the first dome tent. By 1975 North Face had come up with the first geodesic design. As camping equipment changed and became more compact so did food, through the technology of freeze-drying. Freeze-dried foods were compact and easy to prepare.

The next issue to be tackled was water purity. Many diseases can be contacted from drinking unclean water from streams or rivers. Until recently disease prevention was limited to boiling water or treating it with foul-tasting iodine tablets. Today, hand-pumped microfiltration systems are used.

As water purification techniques developed, a major breakthrough in water-repellent clothing occurred. In 1969, Bob Gore took some plastic coating, the kind usually used to cover electrical wire, and rapidly stretched it. The result was a thin membrane that repelled water but was still breathable. This meant that campers could be protected from rain on the outside without trapping perspiration on the inside. Gortex material was developed, and by 1976 Gortex gear was available in everything from clothing to sleeping bags.

Today there are numerous companies inventing, testing, and manufacturing new camping gear. Wherever technology leads us it will never change the reasons why we need to camp—whether it is to connect with ourselves, our families, or nature or just for fun!

Victorinox and the Swiss Army Knife Company

In 1886 the Swiss army began equipping every soldier with a regulation general-purpose pocketknife. Up to that time, the standard-issue pocketknife had consisted simply of a single blade and was just one of a whole range of implements the soldier used to look after himself and maintain his

Good camping gear makes for a fine outing in
the woods

rifle. In 1889 the Swiss army adopted a new rifle called the
Schidt-rubin, and it assembled all of the soldier's utensils
into one unit. Accordingly, the Swiss army defined a new
model of multipurpose knife as a rifle accessory. The Swiss
army's specifications for the new accessory were very
detailed.

This pocket knife was officially designated the Soldier's
Knife, model 1890. The Soldier's Knife was very robust and
also relatively heavy. Another knife, the Swiss Officer's, was
a lighter and more elegant version that, apart from the blade,

included a reamer, can opener, and screwdriver. It also had a second small blade and a corkscrew. Thereafter, a man by the name of Elsener began producing other ingenious pocket knives, which he did not identify with numbers but rather with names, such as Student, Cadet, and Farmer.

Many soldiers and civilians used the Swiss Army Knife, and for Christmas fathers would wrap Swiss Army Knives as presents for their sons. I found my Swiss Army Knife under the Christmas tree when I was ten. My dad gave it to me. I still have that knife. There are seven tools embedded in the red casing with the black-and-silver Swiss cross. I used all of the tools then, and I still do now. After Dad died, my son, Scott, received a Swiss Army Knife from me the Christmas he was ten. He still has the knife.

Missouri Rivals the Best of States

Missouri lands and parks offer individuals and families many recreational opportunities. The Missouri Department of Conservation can be proud of its *Outdoor Missouri Map,* which lists alphabetically public lands and indicates the areas that allow fishing, hunting, waterfowl hunting, and primitive camping. Available boat ramps and firearms and archery ranges are marked, as are miles of hiking trails, miles of designated horseback trails, and disabled-accessible parking.

Whether you enjoy hiking, fishing, hunting, camping, boating or viewing wildlife, this map will help you find some of Missouri's most beautiful natural areas. Activities permitted on each area are indicated by letter abbreviations following the road directions. Bright orange locator codes on the map coincide with all areas listed on the back. Each entry includes acreage, directions, and list of activities for every area. Information about state parks' facilities and map coordinates are found on the front of the map. Areas equipped for the disabled outdoor enthusiasts are highlighted in a separate facilities chart.

Special regulations, when applicable, are posted in the area. The types of public lands are indicated on the map by codes:

CA—Conservation Area
WA—Wildlife Area
NA—Natural Area
SF—State Forest
CL—Community Lake

State parks, all of which appear on the map, are owned and managed by the Missouri Department of Natural Resources (DNR). Everyone who uses Missouri's public lands is responsible for knowing and following the rules and regulations published in the *Wildlife Code of Missouri*. A copy of the code is available from the main office of the Conservation Department, from any of its eight regional offices—Northwest, St. Joseph; Northeast, Kirksville; Kansas City, Blue Springs; Central, Columbia; Ozark, West Plains; St. Louis, St. Charles; Southwest, Springfield; and Southeast, Cape Girardeau—or from vendors that sell fishing and hunting licenses, which are regulated by the Conservation Department.

The following offices can provide information on various recreational activities within the state. (See the back of the book for additional sources.)

The Mark Twain National Forest, U.S. Forest Service, 401 Fairgrounds Road, Rolla, MO 65401 (573) 364-4621.

Missouri Department of Conservation, P.O. Box 180, Jefferson City, MO 65102 (573) 751-4115.

Missouri Department of Natural Resources, P.O. Box 176, Jefferson City, MO 65102 (573) 751-3443 or 1-800-334-6946.

Missouri Division of Tourism, P.O. Box 1055, Jefferson City, MO 65102 (573) 751-4133.

Ozark National Scenic Riverways, National Park Service, Box 490, Van Buren, MO 63965 (573) 323-4236.

The Ozark Trail

The Ozark Trail is an ambitious, cooperative project among several public agencies, private landowners, and citizens' groups. It is designed to provide hikers with some of the most scenic and varied landscapes in Missouri. The trail will extend from St. Louis southwestward through the Ozarks and join the Ozark Highland Trail at the Arkansas border. An eastern loop passes through the beautiful St. Francois Mountains region.

About three hundred miles are complete, and when finished, the trail will extend about five hundred miles across Missouri. Completed sections are good for camping and day hiking and for more experienced backpackers. Several sections are open to mountain bicyclists and horseback riders.

The coordinating agency for the trail is the Department of Natural Resources. More information and detailed section maps are available by writing to the Missouri Department of Natural Resources Ozark Trail Coordinator, P.O. Box 176, Jefferson City, MO, or by calling (573) 751-2479.

Camping in Missouri Is as Good as It Gets!

Missouri's forest is something to be proud of. From the southern Ozarks to the northern upland, east and west, the Ozarks offer campgrounds, rivers for float trips, excellent sites for fishing or hunting, trails for biking, historic sites, and scenic drives. Hiking the trails, camping in the forests, or paddling boats along the waterways is the best tonic for those who admire the great outdoors and want to get out into its beauty.

Instead of turning on the same tired television, families have the choice of boating, fishing, hunting, camping, or hiking. They can sing songs around the campfire. For those who like ghost stories, there is no better place to scare yourself. A big basket of s'mores for munching after the all-time favorite meal—hotdogs roasted over the firepit—sets the tone for a perfect campout. First-timers don't have to be afraid.

Author camping during waterfowl season

Learning to put up the tent is also part of the adventure!

Yes, there may be an unexpected rainstorm too. Not being able to get the grudging campfire to flame big and happy can be frustrating, to say the least. So you did not dress warmly enough for cold weather, rainy weather, snow, and ice? Sure, you forgot the proper eating utensils. And how about those mosquitoes, gnats, and flies, which are so big and wanting your blood, your tent, your meal? And you want your mosquito spray, which you can't find in the backpack!

Then there are the barred owl, "Who Cooks for You," and the great horned owl, whose calling wakes you up just when you have finally fallen asleep and scares you half to death.

Don't worry. Owls rarely fly into people's tents.

Camping in Missouri is a pleasure year-round. Hiking through the woods and learning to put up a tent can be an educational experience. Organizations, as well as families, camp together and explore the outdoors. The Boy and Girl Scouts and their troop masters often camp and learn about the woods, glades, and prairies. Camping offers participants opportunities to enjoy many special events, such as singing around the campfire and telling ghost stories that can give you the shivers making you run for the tent, jump onto your cot, and bury your head under your pillow!

Some foods are just made for eating by the campfire. No special tools are needed to make them—except a sharpened stick. However, patience is required while waiting for roasting hotdogs and the scrumptious dessert of mouthwatering s'mores to munch on. If you're feeling adventurous, you can cook fish and even bread on a stick. (See the back of the book for recipes.) Yes, there is always a chance of the unexpected storm. But you know your tent is a worthy home in the boonies. You pitched it in a spot where you will stay safe and cozy.

A table lamp with built-in alarm clock and light-up display can be used at camp and at home. They can be found in wilderness outfitters' stores, or one is available from the Coleman Company. Another good camping product from Coleman is a rechargeable spotlight with red and amber lenses. Lanterns are always helpful. And for cooking, when you can't start the campfire or just want a quicker, more dependable way of cooking, Coleman fuel feeds green camp stoves on many campouts in the boonies.

Dress for the weather. Foul weather can dampen the best plans for camping, but it doesn't have to ruin a campout. I have been with my family when the skies were foreboding. We'd hunker down in the tent, play cards, and listen to the rain pattering on canvas or nylon. Nylon tents are used more than canvas tents these days. However, canvas works well for large numbers of campers like troops of scouts. Pillows are fine if you have the space. Scaled-down sofa pillows from home are just as good or better than bed pillows and take little space.

In primitive camping, campers fend for themselves when it comes to relieving themselves in the woods. Unfortunately, there are people who have little respect for the forests and leave trails of toilet paper and feces along pristine forest trails. Horses also can muck up the forest if their riders are careless. Fecal matter should be buried far from the camp. A garden trowel can be used to bury the waste. Back at camp, a thorough handwashing is best. Rinse off the garden trowel with water and soap. On guided camping trips the guide or guides handle the toilet situation for their clients. They know that a clean "bathroom" makes a good camper who will come again. Those campers who are on their own can take a lesson from the guides. Keep the forest pristine. Only the animals of the land have the right to be animals!

The love of camping hinges on the beasts of the forests. Missouri has its share of mammals. Coyote, gray fox, red fox, mink, muskrat, opossum, raccoon, river otter, spotted skunk, striped skunk, long-tailed weasel, black bear, whitetail deer, and mountain lion can all be found in the state. Game birds are wild turkey, snipe, woodcock, ducks, geese, ruffed grouse, collared dove, mourning dove, ring-necked pheasant, bobwhite quail, clapper rail, king rail, and American coot.

Missouri State Lands for Camping

Bennett Spring State Park—Bennett Springs for trout fishing
Big Lake State Park, Mound City
Busiek State Forest and Wildlife Area
Spokane Cuivre River State Park, Troy
Finger Lakes State Park, Columbia
Harry S. Truman State Park
Warsaw Lake of the Ozarks State Park
Brumley Lake, Wappapello State Park
Williamsville Long Branch State Park, Macon
Maramec Spring Park, Sullivan Montauk State Park, Ashley
    Creek Pomme de Terre State Park, Pittsburg
St. Joe State Park, Flat River Stockton Park, Umber
Table Rock State Park, Branson

Missouri's National Lands

Over two million acres of land in Missouri are owned by the federal government and administered by several agencies. These lands are for the people! Many Missourians and visitors to the state have camped, fished, hunted, and boated near these quiet mountains, lakes and streams, hills, and valleys and in designated wilderness.

Missouri's national lands (listed below) can stir the heart.

Bell Mountain Wilderness
Blue Springs Lake Project, Blue Springs
Bull Shoals Lake Project, Clarence Cannon Dam, and Mark Twain Lake Project
Clearwater Lake Project, Piedmont
Devil's Backbone Wilderness
Eleven Point National Wild and Scenic River
Harry S Truman Lake and Reservoir
Hercules Glades Wilderness
Mark Twain National Forest (includes Ava Ranger District, Cassville, Paddy Creek Wilderness, Piney Creek Wilderness, and Rock Pile Mountain Wilderness)
Irish Wilderness
Long Branch Lake Project, Macon
Longview Lake Project, Lees Summit.

Missouri's Unique Natural Features

Big Spring, located in the Mark Twain National Forest, is one of the country's largest and one of the world's single-outlet springs. Average daily flow is 277 million gallons of water, which gushes 1,000 feet from dolomite cliffs to join the Current River.

Johnson's Shut-Ins, from the Current, or the east fork of the Black River, is "shut in" between walls of a narrow gorge that originated in volcanic eruptions nearly 1.5 billion years ago.

Jeannie Muller and son in front of the campfire, Mark Twain National Forest

Water carved unique shut-ins, chutes, and potholes. The area is named for a former landowner. One of the country's largest, it has a daily flow of nearly 300 million gallons. Hiking trails encompass the shut-ins.

Maramec Spring, a national nature landmark, and the St. James Spring, a base of dolomite bluff, have an average daily flow of 96 million gallons. They are the source of water power for the 1857 Maramec Iron Works, the ruins of which are still visible.

Jeannie Muller at campsite in Mark Twain National Forest

Taberville Prairie, a national natural landmark located in Taberville, is one of the state's largest virgin tallgrass prairies (1,360 acres) and has never been plowed. Typical species of animals and plants include the prairie chicken, bluestem grass, and the now-threatened milkweed. There is a rare prairie stream and a nature trail for hiking.

Taum Sauk Mountain, Taum Sauk Mountain State Park, is the highest point in the state (1,772 feet) named for a chief of the Piankisaws. Accessible by automobile or via the Ozark Trail, a lookout tower provides a 360-degree view. The waterfall and the highest point in the state make a fine day of scouting.

Camp Is a Special Place for Beauty and Recollection

How well you prepare for a camping trip is a reliable predictor of the comfort and enjoyment you will derive. Forgetting a frying pan, spatula, flashlight, or even the tent is a bad deal. Lost time can lead to inconvenience and problems. There is some satisfaction in successful improvisation upon making a discovery that the roll of toilet paper was not packed. But for the most part, forgetting important items is a headache and campers pay the price.

Here are some things to be remember when planning a campout. Not dressing warmly enough for cold weather and unexpected storms can ruin a trip. Remember, you can slip out of your heavy duds if it gets too warm. Forgetting the proper utensils for cooking, insect repellent for mosquitoes, gnats, pesky flies, and no-seeums can make the campout drudgery. To make the best of the outing, be awake and alert to your surroundings when camping.

We will define camping here as a sport where a nylon or canvas duck tent, truck camper, or motor home is the primary shelter. The tent and all related equipment are packed into the car or truck. Because this gear has to be gathered, organized, loaded, and unloaded for each trip, there can be opportunity for error.

Some go-light campers with simple needs keep preparation time to a minimum. They are ready to go on short notice with a minimum of equipment and food. One friend always kept a sleeping bag, nylon tarp (his tent), and cooking gear in his truck. His supply for a three- or four-day stint in the forest comprises canned goods such as beans, soup, fruit, Spam (not bad when fried), tuna, salmon, stew, hash, sardines, chili, and coffee, plus crackers.

This friend is a fine fisherman. He adds fresh fish to the menu every chance he can. The canned goods system is all right for those who can tolerate a steady diet of it. It is impractical for backpacking because of the weight and pack-out litter involved. But food preparation is simple and quick, leaving more time to enjoy hiking, camping, fishing, or hunting.

Making a list of items to bring on a campout can be very helpful. You will want to make your own list and adjust it depending on whether you are tent camping or car camping. To get you started, here is a basic list of items needed for a campout.

Sleeping:

Tent with rainfly and stakes
Ground tarp
Sleeping bag and pad (Pads are more durable and comfortable than air mattresses.)
Backpack and pack cover

Clothing and Footwear:

Rain jacket and pants
Swimsuit
Comfortable boots and camp shoes
Long pants and long-sleeved shirt (regardless of the temperature)
Extra socks
Hat

Cooking:

Jug of drinking water, canteens
Frying pan
Two-quart kettle
Coffee or tea pot
Aluminum foil
Spatula
Plates
Eating utensils
Hand and dish soap

Pot scrubber

Wash basin

Towel

Matches in waterproof container or stove/lantern lighter

Garbage bag

Food bag or basket filled with nonperishable food items

Homemade grub box (holds all food preparation items)

Ice chest or cooler recommended for beverages and an additional supply of ice (Block ice lasts longer than cubed or crushed ice.)

Camp stove with extra fuel canister

Charcoal and lighter fluid

Lubrication oil (small can for stove and lantern)

Pressure pumps

Salt, pepper, and other seasonings of choice

Other essentials:

Lantern and extra mantles for gas lantern

First aid kit

Lip balm

Sunscreen SPF 15+

Sunburn balm

Moleskin for blisters

Medicine for insect bites and poison ivy

Toilet paper

Trowel

Toothbrush and toothpaste

Sunglasses

Flashlight (with extra batteries)

Maps of the camping area

Compass

Money for camping fees

Pocket or belt knife

Deck of cards (or game)

A First Aid Kit Can Keep You on the Trail

Choose a kit that you will pack along on every outing as part of your essential camp gear. Purchase kits for home and for the car or camping. Select kits with complete instructions inside.

Basic Components of a Good Kit

Scissors
Safety pins
Tweezers
Razor blades
Tourniquet
Baking soda
Rubbing alcohol
Antibiotic cream
Burn ointment
Hydrogen peroxide
Gauze pads
Tape
Cotton swabs
Latex gloves
Vaseline
Soap
Antibacterial cleansing wipes
Diarrhea medication (type recommended by your physician),
    Toothache remedy (brand recommended by your dentist)
Aspirin
Water-purification tablets
Adhesive bandages (roll of bandages 3/4-inch wide up to 2
    3/8 inches wide)
Band aids
Thermometer
First aid manual

Keep the contents of the kit organized and in a well-marked, durable, waterproof container that is readily available. Inspect the kit often and restock as needed. Medicine

National Forest Wilderness near Table Rock Lake

cautions: Always apply according to the recommended dosages on the bottle for various ages and weights. Many camping-related ailments can be cured with sleep, water, tea, salt, sugar, aspirin, and kind words.

Camping Legacy

Harrison Brown said, "The machine has divorced man from the world of nature to which he belongs, and in the process he has lost in large measure the powers of contemplation with which he was endowed."

When Thoreau built his cabin on the north shore of Walden Pond, he sought kinship with the land and a simpler life. He wanted to spend more time thinking and enjoying the free gifts of nature. That was well over 130 years ago, when life was supposed to be less complex.

Now, more than ever, we need our Walden Ponds for weekend sanctuaries and summer retreats. But today, we need them year-round. As we have become an increasingly urban society, we have lost touch with nature. Kids suffer the most from this loss, whether they realize it or not.

What's left for kids? Highly structured, adult-supervised court and field sports that reward the physically gifted and encourage intense competition. Young people are locked into the artificially controlled refinements of indoor living. They are knowing victims of climate-controlled bondage and the hazardous city attitude. All spare moments must be filled to the brim with physical or mental activity.

Tent-camping is a good way to develop or rekindle a lasting relationship with the natural world, and spring is the best time to start. Choose a spot in the Mark Twain National Forest. Primitive camping offers the finest rewards. Developed campgrounds that offer a variety of conveniences and services for a fee attract the most people. The pleasures of pure camping are lost in crowds, noise, and people-management restrictions. When it comes to solitude, you might be better off in your own backyard.

Erect a roomy, waterproof, insect-proof lodge with a great view in less than twenty minutes. The very act of pitching a tent is uniquely satisfying. Slow down. Leave the speed shifting at home. Take pleasure in pitching the tent. And help with camp cooking; end a division of small simple chores. Observe how children fit naturally into outdoor living without manufactured entertainment. Camp for camping's sake. Welcome the rain if it comes. You can stay dry and warm. There is no finer drumming than the relaxing beat of rain drops on nylon or canvas roofs. Study the trees. Listen to the birds. Leave the radio and battery-powered television at home along with the cell phone. Natural spring serenades are brilliant.

Modern tent-camping equipment has made outdoor living more acceptable, practical, comfortable, and enjoyable. Sewn-in nylon floors keep out insects, snakes, and rain. Lightweight, modern tents are easy to erect even for novices.

Camp cooking

They are designed with aluminum or fiberglass frames. Flex poles keep fabric taut enough to resist wind and rainfall. The tent, plus sleeping bags, mattress pads, ice chest, lantern, stove, and cooking gear take up relatively little storage room. With minimal care, equipment will last twenty years or more. Buy name-brand gear; you will never regret it!

The success of the camping family is based on the unwritten campers' code of equality. That means chores are divided as equally as possible among adults and kids. Nobody gets waited on. Mom is not supposed to be stuck with all the dirty

Camp cooking

work. Men share the cooking and dishwashing duties. So do the kids.

Keep meals simple and fun with an eye toward using as few pots and utensils as possible. A tasty breakfast idea makes the cooking as much fun as the eating. Frozen waffles can be toasted over the fire or camp stove. Hot dogs or Polish or Italian sausage held over the fire on long-handled barbecue forks or cooked on top of wire grills are just a few of the tasty, easy-to-fix options for camp. Some recipes are included in the back of the book.

The tent-camping experience takes effort. But the satisfaction of living comfortably with nature stimulates the senses.

When you pass camping skills to youngsters, you give them a lifetime gift. Learning together builds confidence and a treasury of memories.

Ode to a Campfire

I sit at your side and you warm me.

You soothe my aches and sweeten my senses.

Your glow mesmerizes and your crackle lulls me to sleep. You are more than fire. You are friend.

You keep me company in the black of night. You are my beacon in the wilderness.

Your sweet hickory breath saturates me.

I feed you sticks of strength.

You live through me and I through you.

Those who bask in your radiance are mellowed. Oh, the tales you ignite and witness.

Your spirit ascends on a rising column of smoke. And when you flicker and die, part of me dies too. For your tongue is unique and gives special joy. And when your final ember glows no more,

I bid you farewell.

Charlie Farmer

Winter Camping Tips

In Missouri, most campground facilities, whether public or private, are shut down in the winter. Don't sweat it! There is a lot of fine camping and trekking from October through January. If you do not have a winter-weight sleeping bag, stuff one summer bag into another for extra loft and warmth. Use foam pads under the bag for insulation against the ground. Use an extra ground tarp on the inside floor of a nylon tent for a cold barrier. Choose winter campsites that offer protection from the wind and are in a spot where the sun shines the longest during the short winter day. Long underwear (wool, polypropylene, or Thermax) serves nicely for sleeping. Wool is a good insulator and, unlike other materials, retains warmth even when wet. Wear a wool stocking cap for sleeping when it is really cold. In extreme cold weather, leather boots, wet with perspiration, can freeze. Your best bet is to wear rubber-bottom, leather-top boots large enough to be worn with thick wool socks or felt liners. They are waterproof and comfortable.

In the Ozarks, cold or freezing rain, more than snow, is a threat to staying warm and dry. Pack good-quality rain gear, both parkas and pants for adults and kids. Insulated overalls for kids work well. They take the brunt of punishment (mud and moisture) during the day while protecting the second layer of clothing and can be removed and dried at night.

Pack along charcoal lighter fluid for starting the wood fire. Wet wood is common in winter. Keep a winter campfire going by using a high-quality folding camp saw to cut dry downfall (no live trees) to feed it.

Remember to douse your campfire before leaving the campsite. Leave some camp water to pour on the fire. Make sure the fire is soaked with water and then buried so the embers are dead-out. Safety matters! Good campers would never want to burn down a pristine forest. Smokey Bear signs are still hanging in most pristine forests. The reminder to douse matches and campfires before heading home is still the best!

More Safety Tips for Campfires

Clear area of debris before building the fire.
Avoid building the fire beneath overhanging branches.
Avoid green wood, and stack your wood away from the firepit.
Do not build the fire near the tents.
Do not leave the fire unattended.
Do not store fuel (or operate your cook stove) near the campfire.
Keep a bucket of water and a shovel near the firepit.
Remember that you can use water and dirt to put out a fire: pouring water on the fire cools it; throwing dirt onto the fire cuts off oxygen.

Author uses his backpack as a backrest

Hot soup, tea, coffee, hot cider, and cocoa plus high-energy snacks and food should be well-stocked and used in winter menus. Rig a waterproof tarp or shelter separate from the tent for cooking, eating, or lounging in bad weather. Keep the tent's inside dry and clean.

Pack your camera, and keep it inside your sleeping bag or parka so it doesn't freeze. You can get some good shots in winter. Wild animals are more active, and they are visible and concentrated in winter.

Turkey hunters canoeing back to camp

Boating Missouri's Streams, Rivers, Lakes, and Ponds

"Every stream in Missouri has its own character. The Big Piney is special," drawled Butch Robison in pure Alabama-ese. This reverent declaration from my longtime friend and transplanted southerner took me by surprise. Butch, who has lived in Ozark for fifteen years, is no fan of flat water. He likes thunder under the hull and spray in his face. Butch and friends have driven night and day to play chicken with South Carolina's frisky Nantahala River. He has tackled the Chattooga that broke Burt Reynolds's canoe in two in *Deliverance*. And his idea of Ozarks heaven is flooded, frothing Swan Creek fresh from a deluge.

But Robison is not only a thrill seeker. There is ample heart and compassion riding in his Old Town canoe. Scenery, water quality, wildlife, and camaraderie make his trips memorable and worth the long drives, shuttles, hitchhikes, minimal sleep, and missed meals. The sweet music and caress of the streams' currents flow in his veins. "I bet the Finley looked like this once," he lamented ironically.

I had thought the same thing after putting in at Mason Bridge access. The Big Piney from put-in to take-out at Slabtown was clear, deep, full of water, and begging to be fished. Oz Hawksley, author of *Missouri Ozark Waterways*, describes the largest tributary of the Gasconade River as one of the best fishing streams.

He continues to describe the Big Piney as especially good in its upper and middle reaches, where one can view spectacular limestone bluffs topped with pines. There is also a good chance to see wild turkey. Numerous good-sized, beautiful springs feed the river so that it is floatable throughout the summer except in especially dry years.

Butch's nine-year-old daughter, Christal, and my nine-year-old son, Scott, enjoyed being with us on this float trip. There were a couple of spots during our nine-mile float where we scraped bottom. We selected a stretch of the north-flowing river that coursed entirely within the boundaries of the Mark Twain National Forest. With few exceptions, the stream and her corridor remain unspoiled and undeveloped. A few parcels of riverfront land still exist, and some spots are posted with no trespassing signs. But for the most part, floaters and campers have free rein.

Gravel bars along that stretch are not as numerous as in some streams like the Current and Jacks Fork. There are enough good streams to allow a liberal choice of places to pitch a tent, build a campfire, and unwind. Several times during the float, I thought of Big Piney's potential for quality deer and turkey hunting camps. The idea was reinforced when a hen turkey flew from one side of the stream to the other, about twenty yards in front of Scott. Then the rest of us witnessed a different turkey making a similar crossing. It was not until we drew close to Slabtown that we saw other paddlers using the river. I found the solitude surprising for a summer Sunday and imagined the contrast of canoe traffic on the bustling Current River.

The forward boats picked out wonderful swimming holes, and handy gravel bars invited us for a picnic. The picnic lunch was just fine. Deviled eggs, watermelon, and all the goodies tasted superb on such a glorious day. We vowed to return for the colors of autumn.

We passed a pair of boats, each carrying two fishermen. They were using live minnows weighed with split shot to ply the sweet spots. They had done well. Smallmouth bass over twelve inches and chunky, mottled goggle eye (rock

Jeannie Muller with canoe, Table Rock Lake

bass) adorned their metal stringers. Scotty was outfishing me by an embarrassing margin. Goggle eye, bass, and horny-head chubs fell regularly from his 1/32-ounce brown marabou jig. The chubs were about eight inches long and attacked the leadheads like bass. Not wishing to taste fillet of chub, Scott released them. Christal watched Scott catch six or seven in a row.

"Scotty sure knows how to catch 'em," she exclaimed, look-ing squarely into my eyes. "Have you caught any?"

I made a silly face to disguise my chagrin and shook my head. Christal grinned sheepishly.

Float Trip Checklist:

Well-fitting life jacket
Water, water, and more water
Snacks
Resealable bag for trash
Hat
Sunglasses with tether
Sunscreen SPF 15+
Shorts or lightweight pants
Long-sleeved shirt
Swimsuit
Windbreaker or rain jacket
Shoes that can get wet (Sandals with secure straps work
    best.)

Houseboat Heaven

Imagine this: a forty-three-foot houseboat, complete with a microwave oven and hot shower, tucked into a secluded cove on Table Rock Lake. Open the glass sliding doors, fore or aft, grab a fishing rod, and cast for crappie or bass. Enjoy a serenade provided by a pair of barred owls. Watch the mist rise off still waters as the sun peeks over an Ozark ridge carpeted with oaks and cedars. The aroma of fresh-brewed coffee, blended with smoked bacon, drifts onto the forward deck. Breakfast is shared among two families—four adults and four children.

The boat is called a "10 Sleeper" model, one of several sizes. Our water camper has two bathrooms and a second level penthouse that makes life onboard, with a crew of eight, quite comfortable. The kids, who range in age from eight to thirteen years old, have fallen in love with the cushioned floor of the penthouse. They play Monopoly, weave braided wristbands, and hold their secret meetings. The accommodations are well designed for sleeping and feature plenty of storage space.

Author and Bob Whitehead canoeing Jacks Fork

If you think that a houseboat is an adventuresome way to spend a weekend or week-long vacation, you're right. In fact, I cannot imagine a better base camp for fishing, swimming, and exploring. Rentals are available in "4-Sleeper" models all the way up to forty-six-foot boats that sleep ten to sixteen.

Table Rock Lake qualifies as a near-perfect houseboat lake because of its abundance of deep water coves that provide seclusion, windbreaks, captivating scenery, and good fishing and swimming. There are enough marinas and gas stops to

Off on a fishing trip to Stockton Lake

stock supplies and keep the fuel tank filled. Houseboats, because of their size, shape, and wind resistance, are gas guzzlers, so short trips are generally recommended over long-distance cruising destinations.

Lyle Schoning and Charles Julian, of Tri-Lakes Houseboat Rentals and Sales in Kimberling City, gave our crew a twenty-minute orientation on boat operation before our 5 p.m. Friday departure. The boat, equipped with a quiet jet engine (no lower unit hang-up in shallow water), is simple to operate. The captain's cockpit and instruments consist of power stick and a forward-neutral-reverse gear-shifting lever. It was demonstrated how the boat can be turned by applying power in neutral gear. Backing the boat is similar to backing a trailer. The steering wheel backs the boat to the left when turned to the right and vice versa. The rest of the orientation dealt with the operation of gas stove, refrigerator, furnace, air conditioner, marine toilets, and engine blower. On our first night out, in early April, the heat from the furnace felt good!

All hands, including the kids, took turns at the wheel. The thrill of running a forty-three-foot "ship" is a memorable one. Even though none of us had operated a houseboat before, running and mooring the boat went smoothly. We carried a twelve-foot Coleman "Crawdad" johnboat on the houseboat. That little skiff, powered by an electric motor, was easy to launch from the main deck and proved to be perfect for plying the shoreline of Mill Creek and Indian Creek Coves with fishing gear. We also explored the narrow, clear creeks with the small boat.

According to Mona and Steve Fennema of Tri-Lakes, the peak of the houseboat rental reason on Table Rock begins Memorial Day weekend and lasts through the summer. However, spring and fall seasons present attractive options for those who want to experience the birth of nature and the beauty of seasonal color from the comforts of a floating home. Rental houseboats are equipped with everything for food preparation, eating, and sleeping. The renter adds food, drinks, and personal items. Houseboat adventuring becomes a reality. House-boating Ozark lakes is habit-forming!

Occurrence at Marker 13

Our family tent-camped in a secluded cove on Table Rock Lake in the Mark Twain Forest. I hunted turkeys Saturday and Sunday morning, while the rest of my family fished. Much of the two days were spent fishing for crappie, catching frogs, and hiking some of the numerous trails around camp.

Toward evening, we quietly patrolled an old logging road in hopes of rousting a gobbler. While the toms were silent, we did manage to walk up on a hen turkey and slipped within thirty yards of doe whitetail. Heading back to camp in the dim light of dusk, we could hear the shrill notes of spring peepers and chorus frogs come to life.

In the glow of the camp lantern and the dancing flames of a small fire, we cooked supper, ate, and relived our daylight adventures. Around midnight, a deer sounded alarm snorts just behind our tents. The animal was so close, I could hear its steps. The rest of the family was asleep. The communion with nature was near-perfect. Little did I know then that Mother Nature would throw us a mean and unexpected curve, testing our mettle, before the trip ended.

Perhaps we lingered at camp a bit too long Sunday afternoon. Dark, gray clouds were stacking in the west. My son, Scott, talked me into bow fishing for the carp that boiled along the shallow mud banks. In the back of my mind, I thought about the five-mile boat trip back to the Cape Fair marina.

We had a lot of gear to pack—camping equipment, shotguns, fishing tackle, and four persons. The boat was nothing fancy, a fourteen-four johnboat that does fine under normal loads and in calm water. We no sooner had the boat loaded and were ready to push off than the first rain drops began to fall.

Rain gear kept us dry as we motored out of the cove. There was nothing to worry about, at least not yet. The drops were increasing in intensity, but they were falling vertically. There was only a light chop on the lake's surface. All of us wore PFDs—personal flotation devices.

Heading out of the protected cove and into a main channel, we found the wind much stronger and the rain falling even harder. I wished the boat had more freeboard and a bigger engine. We could have easily made it back to the dock. We motored another mile bucking strong headwinds and heavy, slanted rain.

The point at marker 13 was in sight. Around the bend was the main lake channel, and I could see that whitecaps were flashing angry faces. The decision was mine, and it had to be made quickly: "Do we make a run for the marina and the prospects of getting home sooner? Or do we wait out the storm?" I headed for a shallow cove on the lee side of the point. Water was getting deeper in the bottom of the boat. It would need bailing out. I headed to shore.

We slid the boat up onto the bank and headed for a cluster of cedars that offered some protection from the deluge. I felt I had made the right choice. The storm raged for the next hour. In the meantime, we rigged a plastic tarp from the

Johnboat, Jacks Fork

cedars that shielded us from the rain. In our camp box, we had charcoal, lighter fluid, and matches. The kids gathered cedar "twiggies" that were relatively dry. We built a mound of them under the tarp, and soon we had a small but physically and mentally warming fire glowing. A downfall log served as a bench. We fed the fire small sticks to keep it going. The wait was cozy. We talked about survival situations.

"You think we could have made it back, Daddy?" Brittany, my daughter, asked. "I'm glad we did this," I told her.

"Do you thing we'll make it home in time for Disney

World?" "We'll see," I responded.

The rain had slowed so that it was barely dimpling the lake's surface when I used a plastic gallon milk jug (cut off at the top) to bail out the seven or eight inches of water that had accumulated inside the boat. We made it back to the marina just before another storm front hit and made it home for Disney!

In the morning we hung out our clothing and gear to dry. The kids went to school. The boat was in the driveway, and I was content with the decision made at marker 13.

Camp Cooking

Food Storage and Cooking Tips

Freeze meat before putting it in the cooler. It will keep longer, and it will help keep other foods cold.

Check ice often and replenish as needed to keep food cold. Remember that block ice lasts longer than ice cubes.

Store all cooler items in watertight bags or containers.

Taking along a separate cooler for drinks will help limit the number of times the food cooler must be opened.

Be sure the handles on pans are fireproof if pans will be used over a campfire.

Use pans as mixing bowls and cut down on the cooking equipment needed.

Putting liquid soap on the outsides of pots and pans before putting them over the fire makes cleanup easier.

Put a pan of water on the stove or over the coals while you eat so it will be ready when you are ready to wash dishes.

Whether you're cooking on a camp stove or over a camp-fire, here are some easy and tasty suggestions for your next camping trip.

Breakfast

One-Dish Breakfast

3 sausage links
3 eggs
1 small potato
1/4 cup shredded cheese
3 tablespoons milk

Cook sausage and cut into small pieces; set aside. Dice the potato and cook in the sausage drippings. Drain. Beat eggs and milk; add to potato. When almost set, add sausage and cheese and cook until cheese melts.

Breakfast in Foil

couple strips bacon
1 or 2 potatoes, sliced
some chopped onion
butter
salt and pepper
cooking spray or oil
1 square heavy-duty aluminum foil

Spray one side of the foil with cooking spray or rub it with oil. Lay bacon strips on foil. Top with potato slices and chopped onion. Season with salt and pepper and put a pat of butter on top. Wrap foil securely. Cook over hot coals.

Bread on a Stick

fresh or frozen bread dough (can substitute a tube of biscuits or
   crescent rolls)
butter
jelly or jam
green sticks (about 1 inch in diameter)

If bread dough is frozen, thaw first. Cut dough into strips 10
to 12 inches long. Starting at the end of the stick, wrap the
dough around the stick in a spiral fashion, leaving space
between each turn so that the heat can reach all parts of the
dough. Pinch the ends of the dough against the stick. Heat
the dough over hot coals for 15 to 20 minutes until the dough
is golden brown. Slip it off the stick and serve with butter and
jam or jelly.

Lunch or Supper ◎　　◎　　◎　　◎　　◎　　◎　　◎

Coffee Can Stew

1/4 - 1/2 pound hamburger or stew meat
2 small potatoes
2 carrots
1 small onion
1 clove garlic
salt and pepper
butter or oil
any seasoning blend you like
1 large coffee can
1 square heavy-duty aluminum foil

Put a bit of oil or butter in the bottom of the coffee can. Peel
and dice potatoes, carrots, and onion and put them in the
coffee can. Add the meat and seasonings. Top with a little
more butter or oil. Cover coffee can tightly with foil. Set in
coals to bake for about an hour or until meat is done and
vegetables are tender.

Fish on a Stick

This recipe works with trout, bass, sunfish, and bluegill.
You'll need green sticks or grilling forks.

Start the fire at least 30 minutes before cooking, and let the fire burn down to coals. Cut fish into large pieces. Thread the fork or a sharpened end of the stick through a piece of fish. Hold it over the coals, exposing the thickest part to the most heat, and slowly cook. When the fish flakes at the thickest part, it's done. Remove from the stick and eat. (Have extra pieces of fish handy in case some fall into the fire.)

Desserts

Baked Apples

1 medium apple
1/2 - 3/4 teaspoon cinnamon sugar
butter
1 square heavy-duty aluminum foil

Core the apple, being careful to leave some of the bottom intact. Place the apple on the square of foil, and sprinkle with cinnamon sugar. Add a dab of butter to the center. Wrap the apple securely in foil. Cook in the coals for 15 to 25 minutes. The apple is done when it yields to pressure. (Be sure to wear gloves!) Open the foil and let the apple cool a little before serving.

Little Fruit Pies

1 can fruit pie filling
1 tube biscuits (large ones work best)
butter
cinnamon sugar

Roll out the biscuits; put spoonful of filling in the center of each one; fold over the biscuits and crimp edges. Heat butter in frying pan. Fry pies on low to medium heat until golden brown and done through. Remove pies from pan and sprinkle with cinnamon sugar. (Be careful; filling will be hot.)

Snack ◉ ◉ ◉ ◉ ◉ ◉ ◉ ◉

Campfire Popcorn

popcorn
oil
butter
salt
large square heavy duty aluminum foil
stick

Tear an 18-inch-square piece of aluminum foil. In the center put 1 teaspoon of oil and 1 tablespoon of popcorn. Gather first the corners and then the edges of the foil to make a pouch. Leave plenty of room for the popcorn to expand. Tie the pouch to a stick and hold the pouch over the hot coals. Shake constantly while the popcorn pops. When it's done, unwrap carefully and add butter and salt.

For More Reading

If you want a general guide to fishing, *Fishing for Dummies* by Peter Kaminsky (Foster City, Calif.: IDG Books Worldwide, 1997) explains the subject in detail. For information on fishing for bass, you might try *The Complete Guide to Finesse Bass Fishing,* by Michael Jones (Canyon Lake, Calif.: McGrady Media, 1991). For ordering information call 800-782-2393. For more information on trout, check *Fly Fishing for Trout in Missouri* by Chuck Tryon (Rolla, Mo.: Ozark Moutain Fly Fishers, 1999), or *Fishing the Missouri Trout Parks: A Streamside Guide to Bennett Spring State Park, Maramec Spring Park, Montauk State Park, and Roaring River State Park,* by James C. Washabaugh (Jefferson City, Mo.: Capitol City Publishing, 1997).

Monte Burch's *Pro's Guide to Fishing Missouri Lakes* (Humansville, Mo.: Outdoor World Press, 1986) provides information specific to Missouri as does C. M. Cooper, C. S. Cooper, and G. D. Phillips's *Cooper-Martin's Guide to Missouri Fishing* (n.p.: Cooper-Martin Publications, 1983), which includes photographs of and information on the fish an angler will find along with county maps and maps of the large lakes and reservoirs, although some of the information in both books is dated.

A variety of publications are available from the Missouri Department of Conservation, such as "Muskies in Missouri" (a pamphlet). You can order them directly from the department, but first check the department's website if possible at

www.conservation.state.mo.us. It is packed with information. Some publications, such as *A Summary of Missouri
Fishing Regulations,* are updated yearly. They are available
from the department, on the website, at checking stations, or
from the vendors that sell fishing licenses. Also readily available is the *Wildlife Code of Missouri: Rules of the Conservation
Commission.*

A Sand County Almanac, by Aldo Leopold (New York:
Oxford University Press, 1949), is a classic on the environment that every lover of the outdoors should read. Excellent
information specific to the state can be found in the *Conservation Atlas—A Guide to Exploring Your Conservation Lands*
and the *Outdoor Missouri Map* from the Missouri Department of Conservation. Searchable versions are available on
the department's website. Some websites with good general
information on the nation's parks and on outdoor recreational activities are the National Park Service, www.nps.gov,
the U.S. Forest Service, www.fs.fed.us, the U.S. Fish and
Wildlife Service, www.fws.gov, and a general guide to recreational activities on federal lands, www.recreation.gov.

Trout Unlimited, www.tu.org, and Ducks Unlimited,
www.ducks.org, both provide good information within their
specialized areas.

Records of North American Big Game is published by and
available from the Boone and Crockett Club. If you're hunting waterfowl, Steve Smith's *Hunting Ducks and Geese: Hard
Facts, Good Bets, and Serious Advice from a Duck Hunter You
Can Trust* (Mechanicsville, Penn.: Stackpole Books, 2003) was
first released in 1984 and has remained popular. The 2003
edition has been updated. *Birds of Missouri: Their Distribution
and Abundance* by Mark B. Robbins and David A. Easterla
(Columbia: University of Missouri Press, 1992) describes the
status and migration patterns of the state's birds. For help in
identifying birds you might see on a camping or hunting trip,
the Peterson guides offer detailed drawings and descriptions,
the Audubon guides offer photos. The Missouri Department
of Conservation has information on hunting waterfowl on its
web site under www.mdc.mo.gov.hunt/wtrfowl/info/seasons.

If you're interested in information on retrievers, the North American Versatile Hunting Dog Association (NAVHDA) www.navhda.com is a good source.

For more information on the National Rifle Association's Women on Target Program, go to www.nra-sign-up.com/womenontarget.htm.

Boaters should check out Oz Hawksley's *Missouri Ozark Waterways,* and *The Floater's Guide to Missouri* by Andy Cline (Helena, Mont.: Falcon Press, 1992).

For more information on camp cooking, there are *The Outdoor Oven Cookbook* by Sheila Mills (Camden, Me.: Ragged Mountain Press, 1997), Dian Thomas, *Recipes for Roughing It Easy* (Cincinnati, Ohio: Betterway Books, 2001), and Linda White, *Cooking on a Stick: Campfire Recipes for Kids* (Salt Lake City, Utah: Gibbs Smith Publishers, 1996).

About the Author

A full-time writer, Charles J. Farmer specializes in accounts of outdoor adventures for the *Springfield News-Leader*, as well as for various magazines. He is also the cohost of the popular radio program *Outside Story*. He is the author of *Unspoiled Beauty: A Personal Guide to Missouri Wilderness*, and he wrote the introduction for *Images of the Ozarks*, both available from the University of Missouri Press.